296.832
H35   Hecht, Michael.
          Have you ever asked
      yourself these questions?

DATE	ISSUED TO

296.832
H35   Hecht, Michael.
          Have you ever asked
      yourself these questions?

Temple Israel Library
Minneapolis, Minn.

Please sign your full name on the above card.

Return books promptly to the Library or Temple Office.

Fines will be charged for overdue books or for damage or loss of same.

DEMCO

HAVE YOU EVER
ASKED YOURSELF
THESE QUESTIONS?

HAVE YOU EVER ASKED YOURSELF THESE QUESTIONS?

A GUIDE TO TRADITIONAL JEWISH THOUGHT

by

Michael Hecht

SHENGOLD PUBLISHERS, INC.
NEW YORK CITY

Library of Congress Catalog Card Number: 75-163738

Copyright © 1971 by Torah Perpetuation Foundation
All Rights Reserved

SHENGOLD PUBLISHERS, INC.
45 WEST 45TH STREET, NEW YORK, N.Y. 10036

PRINTED IN THE UNITED STATES OF AMERICA

Dedicated to

MILTON LEVY ז״ל
whose vision and tireless
devotion brought
this book into being.

PREFACE

For nearly ten years I have been privileged to teach
Talmud at Yeshiva University High School. During that
time I have become convinced that many of us involved in
Jewish education have, at least in one respect, failed our
students. All too often the fundamental philosophic and
quasi-philosophic principles of Judaism—the *hashkafa* of
Yahadut—are glossed over as if through some magical osmotic
process the student will unconsciously absorb them. This is
a luxury which we can ill afford. Many unarticulated but
nevertheless very real questions remain unanswered and,
therefore, continue to plague students and occasionally to
undermine their faith.

This book is designed to correct this situation. In each of
the forty-eight lessons, questions are posed—questions which
trouble students of all ages—and are then answered in a non-
dogmatic manner. Throughout the volume I have attempted
to avoid two potential hazards. First, a watered-down, insipid
version of Judaism, designed to accommodate prevalent
scientific and secular thought, has been shunned. The
eternal truths of authentic, halachic Judaism must be forth-
rightly asserted. If these truths do not happen to jibe with
the currently fashionable views, that is no concern of ours.
But at the same time, I have attempted not to lose sight of
my audience. The approach and method so appropriate to
the nineteenth century Lithuanian pupil will simply not do
for the very different problems of the twentieth century
student.

A Teacher's Guide which supplements the basic text with

additional material, much of it relevant selections from the Talmud and its classical Commentaries, has been provided to enable the teacher and general reader to augment the discussion. A feature of this book is an attempt to systematically incorporate relevant passages from our prayers into the lessons. The study of the Siddur, the Jewish prayerbook, has curiously been neglected at all levels of Jewish education. Nevertheless, the Siddur is a veritable treasure house of Jewish belief. Pedagogically, the familiarity our students have with Jewish prayer makes it an excellent vehicle to reinforce the themes of these lessons.

A preface of this sort would not be complete without an acknowledgment of its author's extensive debts. First and foremost to Milton Levy z.l., past president of the Torah Perpetuation Foundation, in whose memory this book has been dedicated. He first conceived the possibility of this project, and his enthusiasm and support made this volume feasible. Thanks must also be extended to colleagues at Yeshiva University, too numerous to mention by name, and certainly to my students with whom many of the ideas contained in this book were developed; to Moshe Sheinbaum, president of Shengold Publishers, who guided this neophyte author through the maze which led to the publication of this volume. Last, and certainly not least, to Rabbi David Cohen who read the manuscript and whose scholarship and character were a source of guidance and inspiration.

CONTENTS

LESSON 1

CREATION: ACCIDENT OR PURPOSEFUL

Ever since the beginning of mankind, men have speculated about the origin of our universe. Essentially, this speculation has resulted in two radically different approaches to explain the existence of the world. These can conveniently be called the atheistic approach and the religious approach. It is our job to examine these theories, and to understand the implications of each, so that we may be in a position to decide which one more adequately solves the perplexing mystery of life itself.

THE ATHEISTIC APPROACH — The ancient Greeks (Plato) proposed a theory that everything in the universe has come about by chance. To this very day, many educated people still accept this theory.

Before we analyze the atheistic view, a simple demonstration of the enormous numbers which are involved when we deal with chance is in order.

QUESTION 1 — Suppose you take ten pennies and mark them from 1 to 10. Put them in a box and shake them well. Now try to draw them out in sequence from 1 to 10, putting each coin back into the box after each draw. What do you think your chances of drawing 1 through 10 in sequence would be?

According to the theory that the earth was formed by pure chance, the most popular scientific theory today says that a star just happened to pass close enough to our sun to create terrific upheavals, as a result of which chunks from the sun were flung out into space. These chunks eventually became the planets, including Earth. Yet these same scientists will admit that the odds of two stars passing close enough to each other to bring about such an upheaval is more than 10,000,000 to one against such an occurrence.

QUESTION 2 — But even assuming for the moment that the possibility of such an upheaval can and did occur, does this theory in any way explain how the sun and the other stars came into being?

Obviously, this theory does not attempt to answer how the sun or other stars were formed. In fact no responsible scientist claims that science has succeeded in unlocking the mystery of creation. For every scientific theory of creation starts out with a basic premise, namely, given the existence of some form of basic matter, development of the universe can be theorized. However, the existence of this basic matter is never explained; it is accepted as an article of faith. It should be noted at this point that there is a crucial distinction between the faith of religious man and that of scientific man. The scientist's faith is based upon the realization that he has reached a point beyond which science cannot take him; the faith of religious man, on the other hand, is founded upon revelation, namely, G-d revealed to man certain fundamental truths. Naturally man has neither right nor reason to expect G-d to reveal all of His ways; if mysteries remain that is G-d's will.

Let us next consider some facts about the earth. Take,

for instance, its position in the solar system. If the earth were any closer to the sun, it would be too hot to support any form of life. On the other hand, if the earth were any further away from the sun, it would be far too cold to support life. Remember that according to the atheistic theory, it was pure chance that our earth was located in its present place in the billions of miles of the solar system. The earth rotates on its axis in twenty-four hours or at the rate of one thousand miles per hour. Suppose it turned at the rate of only one hundred miles per hour. Our days and nights would then be ten times as long as they are now and the hot sun of summer would burn up all plant life each long day, and every form of vegetation would freeze to death in such a night. According to the accidental theory of creation, we are very luck that purely by chance the earth rotates as it does. The earth travels around the sun at the rate of 18 miles each second. If the rate of revolution had been 10 miles or 30 miles each second, we would be either too far from the sun, or too close to it, for our form of life to exist. If the atmosphere of the earth was similar to that of many planets, the poisonous gases would destroy all life. On the other hand, if the earth had no atmosphere to protect it from the direct heat of the sun, the rays of the sun would consume the earth. If the moon, which controls the tide of the ocean, was 100,000 miles away from the earth instead of nearly a quarter of a million miles, each day at high tide most of the earth's dry land would be flooded by a great rush of ocean water.

Similar illustrations could be cited again and again to prove our point, but that would serve no purpose. Can any logical, rational man not agree with the conclusion reached by one of the most prominent scientists of our age, Dr. A. C. Morrisson, who wrote: "So many essential conditions are necessary for life to exist on our earth that it is mathematically impossible that all of them could exist in proper relationship by chance on any one earth at one time. Therefore there must be in nature some form of intelligent direction."

QUESTION 3 — Suppose you read a book that has hundreds of pages, telling a story. Could you, by any stretch of the imagination, assume that a bottle of ink spilled and the ink accidentally spread in such a way as to produce the hundreds of pages of writing? Is it any more reasonable to assume that the infinite number of atoms, molecules and particles which make up the world and exist in perfect order and harmony could exist purely by accident?

LESSON 2

CREATION: ACCIDENT OR PURPOSEFUL

(Part 2)

Read carefully the following *mashal* (analogy):

Suppose one day while out for a walk, you found a coin. Naturally, you would consider it an accidental piece of good luck. The next day at the very same time and in the very same place, you once again find a similar coin. You would still consider it an accident. But if the very same thing would occur day after day, you would finally conclude that the coins were placed there by someone. Let us continue. Suppose that at intervals of precisely ten feet, you would find a second coin, a third coin and so on, of exactly the same description as the first. If this would continue for hundreds and thousands of miles, you would be forced to conclude that this is no accident, but the result of systematic planning.

QUESTION 1 – Can you relate this *mashal* to the repeated laws of nature discussed in lesson 1? Try to compare the probability of coins being placed purely by chance at precise ten feet intervals for miles and miles, day after day, with the probability of the continued, precise occurrences necessary to sustain life?

QUESTION 2 — Think for a moment. Can you imagine anything found in your home which was not produced by a maker? Your school? Your city? Does this suggest anything to you about the origin of the world?

The Midrash (*Temurah* 5) in the following story relates how Rabbi Akiva proved G-D's existence with the sort of analysis called for by this question. "A heretic once came before Rabbi Akiva and asked him, 'Who created this world?' He replied, 'The Holy One.' 'Give me a clear proof' the heretic said. Rabbi Akiva then asked him: 'What are you wearing?' 'A garment,' he replied. 'Who made it?' Rabbi Akiva further asked. 'A tailor' was the answer. 'I do not believe you. Give me clear proof.' The heretic answered: 'What do you wish me to show you. Don't you know that the tailor made it?' 'And you don't know that G-D created the world?' responded Rabbi Akiva. The heretic then left and Rabbi Akiva's students asked him for the clear proof. Rabbi Akiva answered, 'My sons, just as the house testifies to the builder, the suit to the tailor and the door concerning the carpenter, thus the world testifies that G-D created it."

QUESTION 3 — Read carefully the first *bracha* in *tefilat arvit*, the evening service. What is the essential theme? In what tense is the *bracha* written? Does this suggest anything of *Chazal's* conception of creation?

This blessing details G-D's role in directing the complex functioning of the universe. G-D causes the seasons to alternate; He controls the course of celestial bodies; He creates day and night. It is particularly striking that the text of the *bracha* appears in the *present* tense. Judaism does not view

G-D as the "Prime Mover" who, at one point in time created the world, established the natural order and then withdrew from active direction of the universe. Rather G-D is an active, present participant in the world's affairs. Nor is G-D's role as an active participant in the world's affairs confined to directing the over-all pattern of the universe. G-D is aware of and cares about the deeds and innermost thoughts of individual men. We shall return to this theme many times in the succeeding lessons, particularly in those lessons devoted to *tefilla*, prayer and *schar v'onesh*, reward and punishment.

QUESTION 4 — Is it logical that the great and glorious G-D, the creator of the universe, should concern Himself with the petty, small deeds and misdeeds of individual human beings?

Certainly human logic does not dictate such a conclusion, but on the other hand, neither does it foreclose the possibility. In fact what would be logical human behavior is totally irrelevant in determining how G-d relates to mankind. What is relevant is that G-d in the Torah has time and time again indicated that He is aware of and reacts to man's deeds. This question which troubles many thinking people is based upon a simple but crucial error, i.e., the ascribing to G-d's knowledge the same sort of limits which are inherent in human knowledge. However, as we shall see in future lessons, there are no limits to G-d's power, activity or knowledge.

LESSON 3

AGE OF THE EARTH

We often read and hear that some scientists claim that the earth is billions of years old. In fact, scientists pushed back their estimate of the moon's age in light of the lunar rock samples brought back to the earth by America's first moon-men. As a result of these recent discoveries, they now place the origin of the moon prior in time to that of the earth.

QUESTION 1 — What year did we usher in this *Rosh Hashanah?* Doesn't there seem to be a contradiction? How can we maintain our calendar in the face of current scientific thought?

In this lesson we shall attempt to reconcile this apparent contradiction. First, we must realize that the claim that the earth is several billions of years old is not a proven fact but only a scientific theory. By definition, a theory is an assumption based upon observable phenomena which to some extent has been verified. In other words, a theory is no better than an educated guess. Like many other theories, the view that the earth is billions of years old is subject to some serious criticism. The accepted method used by science to

18

calculate the age of physical bodies is based on the discovery of radio-active elements, e.g., uranium. These elements gradually transform themselves at a fairly constant rate into lead. Therefore, if a rock is found containing both lead and uranium, the scientist in the laboratory can calculate the amount of time necessary for the uranium to have disintegrated into lead. What are some of the unprovable assumptions which must be assumed in order for this theory to have any validity? First, the rate of speed of disintegration from uranium into lead must have been the same in ancient times as it is today. But that cannot be proven. In fact, it has been showed that in the past two thousand years the intensity of the earth's magnetic field has decreased by 65%. Just as the earth's magnetic field has not been constant, so, too, the rate of disintegration need not have been constant.

QUESTION 2 — Do you know what effect extreme heat and pressure have upon chemical or physical processes? Can anyone imagine the extreme heat and pressure generated during *maaseh bereshit?* Do you now understand why there is no necessary contradiction between a belief that the world was created less than 6,000 years ago and the amount of lead found in rocks?

QUESTION 3 — Does the Jewish counting of time begin from the first second of creation? Is it not possible that we record time from the conclusion of the *sheshet yemai bereshit,* the six "days" of creation? Furthermore, since man was not created until the last "day," is it really proper to consider the *sheshet yemai bereshit* in terms of twenty-four hour days, human days? Is it not conceivable that these "days" might in human terms have actually transpired over enormous periods of time? In general, is the concept of time at all relevant to a never changing G-d? Do you see how this may be an alternate solution to the problem posed in question 1 of this lesson?

There is still one further, and probably best, solution to the problem raised in question 1. The creation described in chapter one of *Bereshit* resulted in a complete, mature world. Adam was created as an adult, not as an infant. The trees were created full-grown with fruit, not as tiny seedlings. The forms of life, e.g., bacteria, which derive their sustenance from rotten old trees were provided with such aged decaying material. This much is clear from even a superficial study of the first chapter of *Bereshit*. (We shall return to this theme in our discussion of miracles.)

QUESTION 4 — Is it not probable that the rocks and other physical matter were also created in a mature fully developed state? Is there any logical basis to assume that the lead we find today in rocks is a result of the decomposition of the original uranium? Is it not at least as reasonable to assume that the original creation produced a mixture of lead and uranium? Do you realize the implication of such an argument?

LESSON 4

EVOLUTION OR CREATION

In the next two lessons, we shall examine the theory of evolution first popularized by Charles Darwin. Our purpose is to consider some of the very real difficulties and unanswered questions which the evolutionary theory has never been able to solve.

Darwin believed that the separate species of plant and animal life developed from one, single earlier form of life. But the origin of the evolutionary process raises a question which science has not yet been able to answer. What was the origin of life on this planet? Until fairly recent times, there was general belief in the occurrence of "spontaneous generation," i.e., that the lowest forms of life could develop spontaneously from non-living matter. But careful experimentation, particularly by Pasteur, showed that this conclusion is scientifically impossible and due to imperfect observation.

J. W. Sullivan, who is commonly known as one of the world's most brilliant interpreters of physics, has written that "the only possible conclusion so far as actual evidence goes" is that the origin of life results from a supernatural, G-dly creative act. We shall quote the following passage from his important work, *The Limitations of Science*: "But since it is a conclusion that seems to lead back to some supernatural creative act [i.e., G-d], it is a conclusion that scientific men find very difficult of acceptance. It carries with it what are felt to be, in the present mental climate, undesirable philosophic implications, and it is opposed to the scientific desire for continuity. It introduces an unaccountable break in the chain of causation, and therefore cannot be admitted as part of science."

QUESTION 1 — You should reread carefully this passage not only for its conclusions but also because it casts light upon the scientific method. Do you realize what has occurred here? In its desire for neat, perfectly logical answers to difficult questions, for continuing links in a chain of causation, science has refused to accept the "only possible conclusion so far as actual evidence goes." What has science proposed as an alternative solution? Do you recognize that this alternative is as scientifically unverifiable as the religious answer and requires just as much an act of faith?

Let us put aside the vexing problem of the origin of the lowliest form of life. How did this microscopic one-cell bit of life develop into man? Darwin proposed a theory of "natural selection" which simply put has two main points. 1) Within any species there are individual differences between members of the same species, and 2) there exists in nature a struggle for existence, with the fittest surviving.

QUESTION 2 — How did these individual variations come about? How were they transmitted to offspring?

QUESTION 3 — Have you ever considered how enormously complicated any single organ of the human body is? As an experiment do some research on how many different things must be perfectly coordinated for sight, or hearing, or the functioning of the heart and circulatory system to function properly. Have you ever paused to consider that the most advanced computer is child's play when compared to the complexities of the human body?

As an illustration of the fantastic complexity and perfect coordination of the human body, let us briefly discuss the process of eating and digestion. Once food is placed into the mouth various types of teeth performing different functions prepare the food for passage into the stomach. The tongue moves the food into proper position. Glands in the mouth secrete saliva which begins the chemical breakdown necessary before the food can be utilized by the individual cells, and makes possible the passage of solid food into the stomach. A complicated process routes the food into the stomach rather than into the lung where it would cause choking. In the stomach other enzymes necessary to further chemically break the food down are secreted, and yet the stomach does not digest itself even though it is made of the same material as the digested food. The food then passes into the intestines where the digestive process is concluded. Bile, secreted by the liver in the proper amount necessary for the particular food, finds its way into the intestines to complete the process. From the intestines millions of canal-like structures take the food to the various parts of the body. Each cell receives the exact quantity which it requires.

QUESTION 4 – Does it seem possible that this magnificently exact, complicated and coordinated process came about purely by chance?

QUESTION 5 — After the waste produced by digestion is evacuated, we are required to recite the blessing of *asher yatzar*. What does the phrase

„אשר יצר את האדם בחכמה"

mean? To what does

„נקבים נקבים חלולים חלולים"

refer?

LESSON 5

EVOLUTION OR CREATION

(Part 2)

In contrast to the theory of evolution which proposes a common ancestor for all living creatures, the Torah teaches us that each species of life is unique. An individual and separate creation by G-D was necessary for each of the different species. This accounts for the great chasm which exists between civilized man and the most advanced animals. Even the most ardent proponent of evolution admits that there is a great difference between the mind of man and the mind of the highest form of animal. According to evolutionary theory which envisages small, imperceptible physical changes, a contrary situation should exist.

This great problem has caused evolutionists to develop the theory of the missing link, a creature which would bridge the gap between ape and man. However, the remains of such a missing link have never been found. It has become such an article of faith among some scientists that in their zeal they have succumbed more than once and loudly proclaimed finds, only to be sorely disappointed when these finds were exposed as gigantic hoaxes. In fact if remains of ape-like men were to be found, it would not produce any problem for Jewish thought. The Midrash (*Bereshit Rabba* 23:6), written more than a thousand years prior to the first fossil finds, teaches that in the age of Enosh, as punishment for having perverted their G-Dly image (*tzelem Elokim*), G-D changed some men into ape-like creatures.

"'And to Seth was born a son called Enosh' . . . Abba Cohen Bardela said, until this point in time all men were created in the image and form of G-D, but at this point the generations deteriorated and some men were created changed in the form of apes. Four things of creation were changed in the days of Enosh the son of Seth . . . the fourth, men's visages were changed to that of apes."

Nevertheless, scientists seem to have arrayed an impressive list of arguments which suggest the theory of evolution. In the previous lesson, we have indicated that the overall theory of evolution is subject to two significant strictures. First, it leaves unanswered the origin of life; second, it appears almost mathematically impossible that the complex higher forms of life could have developed purely by chance without some intelligent guiding force. In fact, some eminent scientists faced with the second criticism have adopted a position midway between the Torah *hashkafa* and that of classical evolution. They admit that an intelligence, i.e., G-D, directs the course of evolution. It should be stressed that such an approach is not acceptable to a Torah viewpoint since it denies the unique creation of individual species.

Let us now consider the specific arguments offered by the evolutionists. Certainly the most famous argument is based on the existence of fossils in various layers of rocks, i.e., strata.

QUESTION 1 — Is it not possible that these fossils were created in the days of creation? Since G-d created the earth in a fully developed state (just as Adam did not first appear as an infant), is it not probable that the earth at the moment of creation contained physical evidence of past geological history which in fact never took place? For example, is it not probable that evidence of the erosion of land by rivers, or piles of limestone formed by the remains of marine life, or even fossils of prehistoric animals were created at the first instant of creation?

QUESTION 2 — Although the human intellect cannot expect to fully comprehend the reason behind any particular command or action of G-d, (e.g., *chukim*) can you think of a possible reason which would explain the existence of fossils?

It is ordinarily a futile exercise to engage in such speculation. Many of G-D's ways are not subject to human understanding. Nevertheless, let us attempt a rationalization for the existence of fossils. In the next lesson we shall see that the world contains many tests of our faith in G-D. If man's faith prevails over the intellectual doubts created by these tests, man is naturally deservant of greater reward than would be his due if no such doubts existed. It is certainly possible that G-D purposefully placed such fossils on the earth as a test of man's faith in G-D the creator.

QUESTION 3 — Assuming that we do not accept this approach, i.e., the fossils were created in the days of creation, is it not entirely conceivable that the fossils are remains of life destroyed in the great flood of Noach's time? In fact, the Torah (*Bereshit* 6:11, 12) declares that one of the basic causes of the flood was the sexual corruption which existed. This of course, would explain fossils of animals unknown to us, since only those species created by G-D survived the deluge.

Eminent geologists have also pointed out certain flaws in the fossil theory. The basic assumption of evolution is that as you proceed from older to younger strata of rocks you find fossils of more complex forms of life. But there is no way of dating the ages of the strata, except by means of the fossils they contain. This brings about a classical example of circular reasoning. Evolution is assumed to show that certain strata are older. Then the development of fossil complexity from old to young strata is used as proof of evolutionary development. In other words, you first assume the very thing you wish to prove, and then go ahead and prove it based on the initial assumption. Furthermore, there are numerous "upside-down" geological areas where more complex fossils are found in deeper and presumably older beds. As pointed out in the beginning of this lesson, another vexing problem for the evolutionists is that no fossil has been found which would serve as the "missing-link" between ape and man.

In summary, it is fair to say that there are many phenomena which testify to planning and creation, and there are others which suggest random evolution. Neither view can be proven. But it is impossible for man to contemplate the enormous complexity and magnificent coordination of nature without feeling the hand of the Creator behind them.

QUESTION 4 — What are the ethical and philosophical implications which flow from the evolutionary theory? Does the theory contain any suggestion of an ethical evolution toward G-D? What is left of the dignity of man? What sort of political theories could and have been based on the "survival of the fittest"?

LESSON 6

MIRACLES

Even a superficial study of the Chumash and Nach reveals many instances of *nissim*, miracles, events which transcend the ordinary rules of nature, and violate the laws of probability. These unnatural events are G-d's way of expressing His *chesed* or providence to mankind in general, and to His people in particular. One question naturally arises. In view of the many miracles found in the Bible, why is it that we in our own day see no such miracles? We shall be concerned with this question in this lesson.

The Ramban (Nachmanides) in his commentary on Chumash raises an important question regarding the story of Noach. Clearly a miracle was involved. No matter how large an ark Noach could construct, it could not possibly hold all the people, animals, and food necessary to sustain them. Therefore, why did G-d burden Noach with the building of the ark, a job which according to Rashi and other commentaries took a full one hundred and twenty years? In response to this, the Ramban offers an analysis which is basic to Judaism's concept of miracles. The Ramban explains that miracles conform as much as possible to the natural order of things. Whatever can be accomplished through ordinary

29

human means is so accomplished. Therefore, in accordance with this analysis, G-d had Noach construct a huge ark so that the ultimate miracle would be minimized, and the human role maximized.

QUESTION 1 — How does Rashi explain the great task of constructing the ark? Why did G-d require Noach to spend more than one hundred years working on the ark?

QUESTION 2 — Assuming that the Ramban's analysis is correct, how can we account for the occurrence of miracles as much as possible within the natural order? Why does G-d not reveal His presence to mankind with continued, open and clear miracles? Why has G-d allowed a world to exist where rational men can deny His existence?

QUESTION 3 — In light of the Ramban's analysis, do you understand why it is so difficult to recognize that a particular unusual event is in fact a miracle? Do you realize why the broader perspective provided by reflection over a period of time is necessary before we are able to identify seemingly unconnected, natural events as forming a pattern which can only be understood in terms of miraculous divine intervention?

LESSON 7

MIRACLES (Part 2)

After considering the Ramban's explanation of miracles presented in the previous lesson, you should have reached some tentative conclusions concerning G-d's reason for concealing His direct involvement in human affairs. G-d does not want man and particularly the Jew to be a robot, mutely obeying His commands. If each morning G-d would have a streak of lightning flash across the sky proclaiming the *shema*, man would have no choice. We would be forced to acknowledge Him. But then we would be no better than robots, and no more deservant of reward. G-d prefers to give man *b'chira chofshit*, free choice, so that if an individual is sufficiently intelligent and astute to make the proper choice and accept G-d and His commandments, that individual will surely deserve the reward which awaits him.

QUESTION 1 — According to traditional Jewish philosophic thought, man is considered occupying a higher place than the angels. Do you now understand why that is so?

We should now recall the Ramban's principle that miraculous events occur as much as possible through natural human means. Let us apply that explanation to contem-

SHABBAT: MORE THAN A DAY OF REST

If there is one fundamental belief of Judaism which distinguishes the orthodox Jew from his non-observant brother, it is the observance of the Sabbath. According to the Torah the key, *ot*, or "sign" established by G-d as testimony to the unique relationship which exists between G-d and His people is the Sabbath. It is therefore not surprising that Chazal throughout the Talmud equate a *mechallel* Shabbat with *oved avoda zarah.* Shabbat is truly the foundation of our faith and one who desecrates the Sabbath tramples on that faith.

What is surprising is the almost total ignorance which even many Sabbath observers have concerning the underlying ideas which make up the philosophic rationale of Shabbat. For many of us Sabbath is nothing more than a long list of do's and don'ts. In this and the following lessons we shall try to uncover these basic concepts. Most important we shall then attempt to relate the halacha, the laws of Shabbat, to the underlying themes and concepts.

Each Friday night immediately before *Shemoneh Esreh,* and again in the *Shemoneh Esreh of Shachrit,* we recite the two sentences from *Shmot:*

„ושמרו בני ישראל את השבת לעשות את השבת לדורותם ברית עולם ביני
ובין בני ישראל אות היא לעולם כי ששת ימים עשה ה' את השמים ואת
הארץ וביום השביעי שבת וינפש."

Let us quote these sentences in translation: "The Children of Israel shall keep the Sabbath, to observe the Sabbath throughout their generations as an everlasting covenant. It is a sign between Me and the Children of Israel forever, that in six days the Lord made the heavens and the earth, and on the seventh day He stopped work and rested."

It is clear from these verses that the purpose of the Sabbath as a day of rest is to commemorate the creation and to acknowledge G-d as the creator of the world.

QUESTION 1 — Since Shabbat commemorates the creation of the world, is there anything which would connect it to Israel more so than to the rest of mankind? Is it comparable to the *moadim*, the festivals which commemorate events in Jewish history? Why then does the law of Shabbat apply only to the Jewish nation and not to the rest of mankind? We know that G-d did give certain commandments to all mankind, viz, *shiva mitzvot bnai Noach*. Why was the Sabbath not included among them?

Man alone of all of G-d's creations was granted the intelligence and ability necessary to control and master nature. These great powers have enabled man to harness the forces of nature, to mold and adapt them to his will. Indeed, the great powers granted by G-d to man, have enabled man to create. But these same powers can be fatally misused; they can cause man to think of himself as the sole creator—responsible to no higher being. Such a man sets himself up as a god; he denies any paramount supreme being.

QUESTION 2 — What practical consequences can be attributed to man's denial of a superior being? What effect on the moral and ethical law results from this view?

QUESTION 3 — How can it be impressed on man, endowed as he is with the power to create, that he is not the supreme creator? How can man be made to recognize that his own creative ability was granted to him by a higher being?

LESSON 9

THE HALACHA OF SHABBAT

In the preceding lesson it was shown that Shabbat was established as a means of impressing on the Jew that G-d created the world and all that is found in the world. The Jew is required to refrain from *melacha*, creative work. This resting from creative work impresses upon the individual that despite his creative powers he is not supreme. Man must give up producing and creating one day a week as a constant reminder that he owes his own creative ability to G-d, the Supreme Creator.

QUESTION 1 — How much work, physical labor, is involved in putting on a light switch or a television set? Granted that Shabbat is a day of rest, but why are we prohibited from doing these simple things which seem to be consistent with a state of rest?

These questions are extremely important for they bother many of us and yet at the same time reveal an almost total ignorance of the true conception of *melacha*. The Torah prohibits *melacha* on Shabbat which is usually translated as work, physical exertion. But this is a totally inadequate and misleading definition of *melacha* and in these lessons that term will not be used.

QUESTION 2 — Does the halacha permit someone to carry within his home a heavy table for a Sabbath meal? A heavy set of books? Do you understand why "work," or "physical exertion" is an improper definition of the halachic term *melacha?*

QUESTION 3 — What then does the Torah mean by the term *melacha?* Review carefully the material in Lesson 7. What function does Shabbat serve? Does this give you a hint of the proper definition of *melacha?*

The Torah (*Shmot* 35:2) itself gives an important clue concerning the proper meaning of *melacha.* It commands the Jews to do all *melacha* necessary to construct the *mishkan* during the six weekdays, but not to do any *melacha* on Shabbat. From these verses *Chazal* deduced that those activities performed in the *mishkan* constitute *melacha* for Shabbat.

QUESTION 4 — How many different *melachot* were actually done in the *mishkan?* How many of them can you identify? Can you discover a thread which unifies the first eleven *melachot?*

A *melacha* actually performed in the *mishkan* is called an *av melacha.* A *melacha* which has essentially the same purpose and is performed in a similar but not exact manner is called a *toladah.* For example, writing with an implement similar to a pencil is one of the *av melachot* found in the *mishkan.* Using a typewriter to produce letters would be a *toladah.* The purpose, i.e., producing letters, is essentially the same whether a pencil or a typewriter is used, and the manner in which the letters are impressed upon the paper is similar but not exact. At this point an extremely important observation is in order. There is absolutely no practical difference between an *av* and a *toladah.* Both are equally considered a desecration of the Sabbath. Both are prohibited *midoraitha,* from the Torah. The penalty which halacha imposes for the performance of a *toladah* is the same as that for an *av*.

QUESTION 5 — Another *av melacha* found in the *mishkan* is kindling a fire. Can you think of an appropriate *toladah* in the category of this *av melacha?*

A careful examination of all the *av melachot* reveals that they cover the whole range of productive and creative human activity. We are now ready, with the help of Rabbi S. R. Hirsch's brilliant analysis, to formulate a unified theme interpreting the concept of *melacha*. We have already shown how Shabbat is designed to testify that G-d is the creator of the world. Man, however, strives to master this creation. In fact the mark of an advanced civilization is the extent to which it has gained control over the natural environment. But the more successful man is in mastering nature, the more apt he is to forget that G-d is the source of his power, to forget that in fact he is totally dependent on G-d.

It is the Jew's task to impress upon himself and thereby on all mankind the recognition of G-d's supremacy. We accomplish this by refraining one day each week from *melacha*, purposeful, constructive, creative human activity. This explains why *midoraitha* a *kilkul*, a purely destructive act no matter how strenuous, is not considered *melacha*. At this point you should clearly understand why a simple act of flicking on a light switch is considered a *melacha*, while a difficult, strenuous labor—even wrecking a house—is not classified as a *melacha*.

LESSON 10

SHABBAT (Part 3)

If we examine the thirty-nine *melachot* prohibited on the Sabbath, we find that one appears to be totally different in character from the remaining thirty-eight. Each of the thirty-eight involves some form of productive or material change in the object acted upon. We can understand why each of these *melachot* is considered a creative act. But the *melacha* of *hotzaah*, "carrying," does not seem to fit into this pattern. Here there is no physical, creative change in the object; there is merely a change of location.

The prophet Jeremiah (Jer. 17:21-27) in his warning to Israel that the future of the Jewish state depended on proper Sabbath observance, also isolates "carrying" from the other *melachot*. "Thus said the Lord: Take heed and carry nothing on the Sabbath day, nor bring anything in by the gates of Jerusalem, nor carry out anything from your houses on the Sabbath day, nor do any other *melacha*, but sanctify the Sabbath day as I commanded your fathers . . . And it shall come to pass, if you obey Me completely, to bring nothing in through the gates of this city on the Sabbath day, but to sanctify the Sabbath, to do no *melacha* thereon then shall there enter in by the gates of this city kings and princes sitting upon the throne of David . . . And this city shall be inhabited for ever . . . But if you will not obey Me in keeping the Sabbath day holy, and not carrying anything when entering in at the gates of Jerusalem on the Sabbath day, then I will kindle a fire in its gates, and it shall devour the palaces of Jerusalem, and it shall not be quenched."

This passage is extremely important for two reasons. It indicates the great stress which the prophet placed on the *melacha* of "carrying." The very destiny of Jerusalem depends upon its inhabitants' observance of the Sabbath. Equally interesting is the grouping of the other thirty-eight *melachot* into one category and the isolating of "carrying" into a separate class.

QUESTION 1 — Can you define *hotzaah?* What two different forms of "carrying" are included within the definition? Do you know the halachic difference between *r'shut hayachid* and *r'shut harabim?*

QUESTION 2 — We recognize the role played by the other thirty-eight *melachot* in acknowledging G-d's role as the creator, the master of the natural environment. But since *hotzaah* involves no creative, physical change, it must play some other role. What is this role? Does it perhaps acknowledge G-d as the master of some other human activity?

We have completed our task of defining the basic concepts of Shabbat, and of showing how the halachic prohibitions known as the thirty-nine *melachot* reflect these underlying concepts. The performance of even one *melacha*-act on Shabbat constitutes an arrogant denial of G-d and His mastery of the world. But since these *melachot* are normal weekday human activity, it is relatively easy for a person to forget and unintentionally perform one of these melachot. In order to guard against such an occurrence, *Chazal* erected *seyogim laTorah*, fences around the law. These *seyogim* are the *gezerot* of Shabbat, the Rabbinic prohibitions which protect the sanctity of the Sabbath. In a later lesson we shall see that the Torah not only authorizes but indeed *commands* the

Rabbis to enact such legislation. For the time being it is sufficient if we merely recognize that such *gezerot* are as binding and obligatory on the individual Jew as the laws actually found in the Torah.

QUESTION 3 — Can you think of *gezerot* which were enacted by the Rabbis to prevent the desecration of Shabbat by the performance of each of the following *melachot*: 1) carrying, 2) writing, 3) tying a permanent knot, 4) planting, 5) kindling a fire?

LESSON 11

THE SPIRIT OF SHABBAT

In the previous lessons we have considered Shabbat as a sign between the creator and each individual Jew that G-d created the world and all that it contains in six days. But there is another aspect to Shabbat which plays an extremely positive human role.

QUESTION 1 — In the beautiful poem *Lecha Dodi* recited Friday evening we say the following verse:

„לקראת שבת לכו ונלכה כי היא מקור הברכה מראש מקדם נסוכה סוף מעשה במחשבה תחלה".

What does it mean? Why is Shabbat referred to as the source of blessing?

The Talmud in Shabbat (10b) tells us that G-d said to Moses before He had revealed the laws of the Sabbath: "I have a precious gift in my treasure house, called the Sabbath, and I desire to give it to Israel." Certainly one aspect of Shabbat as a "precious gift" and a "source of blessing" depends upon the concept of *menucha* which is central to proper Sabbath observance. *Menucha* is much more than merely resting, refraining from physical work. It is a sublime, spiritual state of mind. Six days each week we are involved

43

in the labor and tension of complex human life. On Shabbat we lift this burden from ourselves; the toll which the cares of the weekday take of our physical and mental energy is forgotten. It is a day where we are able to rejuvenate our bodies, our minds, and our souls. It is a day of physical and spiritual contentment.

QUESTION 2 — Can Shabbat have this rejuvenating function if we merely refrain from the performance of *melacha?* In the middle blessing of the Sabbath Mincha Shemoneh Esreh, Shabbat is characterized as *yom menucha ukedusha,* "a day of rest and holiness." *Kedusha* is an integral part of *menucha;* there can be no *menucha* without holiness. Can you think of behavior which although not technically *melacha* destroys the *menucha* of Shabbat?

QUESTION 3 — The following appears in Isaiah (58:13):

‏„וקראת לשבת עונג לקדוש ה'..."‏

Can you translate this sentence? Ask your teacher to discuss what the Talmud (Shabbat 113a, b) derives from it.

Chazal completed their picture of the proper spirit and atmosphere which should prevail during the Sabbath from two attitudes required by the prophet Isaiah, i.e., *kibud* and *oneg.* In this context *kibud* and *oneg* mean more than respect and joy. Shabbat must be eagerly awaited, exact preparations must be made to welcome properly the Sabbath queen into the Jewish home. Down to the last detail it must be apparent that this day is different from the six weekdays. The gleaming candlesticks, the rich Sabbath food, the wine and Challah, the immaculate appearance of the home, the clean white tablecloth, the special Sabbath clothes, the family assembled together at the Sabbath table, leisurely, contentedly eating the meal and singing Shabbat zemirot, even the afternoon nap, all testify to the special magic of a Jewish home on Shabbat. This is the *kibud* and *oneg* required by our sages. Most important of all, with the cares of the mundane forgotten, there is opportunity to draw closer to G-d by the study of His Torah.

LESSON 12

GEZEROT: ERECTING FENCES AROUND THE TORAH

In our discussion of the *halacha* of Shabbat we made passing reference to *gezerot*, laws which are of Rabbinic origin. In future lessons we shall encounter many other examples of laws which are *d'rabbanan*, rather than *deoraita*, i.e., *of Biblical* origin. It is therefore most important that we analyze these Rabbinic laws. Our purpose is two-fold; first, we shall attempt to discover the source from which Chazal derived the authority to establish laws; then, we shall attempt to discover the various factors which motivated the Rabbis to promulgate the *gezerot*. Since we have already studied the laws of the Sabbath, they will be used as a model.

Question 1 — Have you ever heard someone proclaim, "Of course I am a good Jew. I follow the laws of the Torah, but I don't feel bound by the laws of the Rabbis. After all, they were only human beings"? Does such an approach make any sense? Can a person be a good Jew and at the same time not observe the Rabbinic laws?

QUESTION 2 — Do you know that at different periods of Jewish history there were occasional groups, e.g., the Sadducees and one thousand years later the Karaites, who adhered strictly to the letter of the written Bible but denied the *mesorah* or tradition of the Rabbis and the Rabbinic laws? What happened to these groups?

The following sentence appears in *Devarim* (17:11):

„עַל פִּי הַתּוֹרָה אֲשֶׁר יוֹרוּךָ וְעַל הַמִּשְׁפָּט אֲשֶׁר יֹאמְרוּ לְךָ תַּעֲשֶׂה לֹא תָסוּר
מִן הַדָּבָר אֲשֶׁר יַגִּידוּ לְךָ יָמִין וּשְׂמֹאל".

"According to the word of the law which they [the Rabbis] shall teach you, and according to the judgment which they shall tell you, you shall do; you shall not depart from the word which they shall tell you, to the right nor to the left."

It is apparent from this sentence that the Rabbis have the full approval of the Torah to enact those laws which they feel are necessary and proper. In fact the Rambam is of the opinion that every Rabbinic *gezerah* has the force of *deoraitha*. According to the Rambam if a Jew fails to observe a *gezerah*, he not only has violated Rabbinic law but also has transgressed the Biblical

„לֹא תָסוּר מִן הַדָּבָר אֲשֶׁר יַגִּידוּ לְךָ יָמִין וּשְׂמֹאל".

QUESTION 3 — Do you now realize why it is absurd to question Chazal's authority to enact legislation? Prior to the performance of a Rabbinic mitzvah, e.g. the lighting of the Chanukah candles, we recite the following blessing:

„בָּרוּךְ אַתָּה ה' אֱלֹקֵינוּ מֶלֶךְ הָעוֹלָם אֲשֶׁר קִדְּשָׁנוּ בְּמִצְוֹתָיו וְצִוָּנוּ ...".

The Talmud (*Shabbat* 23a) tells us that based on the sentence quoted above, a mitzvah of the Rabbis is considered to have been *commanded* by G-d.

QUESTION 4 — What different types of *gezerot* concerning the laws of Shabbat were enacted by the Rabbis? What types of behavior are prohibited lest they lead to *melacha*?

Before we attempt to classify the various types of *gezerot* enacted there is one further Biblical verse which must be considered.

(ויקרא י״ח:ל׳)   „ושמרתם את משמרתי...".

"And you shall safeguard my charges . . ." This sentence commands the Rabbis to construct *seyogim la Torah*, fences about the law, so that G-d's commandments may not be violated.

Chazal have constructed two types of *gezerot* on Shabbat, two types of acts, which although not themselves *melachot*, could very easily lead to *melachot*. a) Acts which outwardly resemble a *melacha*, and so can easily be confused with them. b) Acts which are linked with *melacha* by habit or which unintentionally but often may lead to a *melacha*.

QUESTION 5 — Can you think of at least several examples for each of the types of Sabbath *gezerot*?

LESSON 13

ACHDUT HASHEM: THE UNITY OF G-D

The most famous and important formulation of the basic philosophic principles of Judaism is found in Maimonides' commentary on the first Mishna of the chapter *Chelek*, the eleventh *perek* of Sanhedrin. Here, the Rambam isolates thirteen *yesodot*, or articles of faith, which make up the essential beliefs of *Yahadut*. The Rambam's Thirteen Principles appear in the Siddur in two forms, in the poem *Yigdal* at the very beginning of *Shacharit* and in prose form at the end of *Shacharit* in the *Ani Maamins*. As we study these principles, you should check both *Yigdal* and *Ani Maamin* for the appropriate formulation in our prayers.

Each day in *Keriyat Shema* we affirm our belief in the unity of G-D, "*Hashem Echad.*" The Rambam after listing as the first principle the belief in G-D, makes *achdut Hashem* the second *yesod*. In your history textbooks you probably have read that the Jews disseminated the concept of monotheism throughout the world. Monotheism is one way of stating in succinct form the Rambam's first two principles, the belief in G-D and the unity of that G-D.

QUESTION 1 — Why is monotheism so fundamental to religion? Does it really make a difference whether man believes in one G-D, or in many gods?

49

When our *Avot*, our forefathers, proclaimed to the world almost four thousand years that G-D is one, it was indeed revolutionary. At that time (and in fact among some contemporary religions) there was a belief in many gods. Each natural phenomenon, e.g., the sun, moon, wind, fire, rain etc., was thought to be under the control of a separate god. Different human events, e.g., birth, death, war etc., were likewise thought to be controlled by separate gods. Naturally, no harmonious pattern controlling human events was thought to exist. The world was pictured as a place of utter chaos with different gods constantly struggling with each other for supremacy. Naturally, there could be no single proper or right or moral code of human conduct. For the appropriate human conduct constantly changed depending upon which particular god was considered to have achieved temporary supremacy. In place of this chaotic view of the human condition, our forefathers introduced the idea of one G-D controlling and guiding all the varied aspects of the universe according to a single divine plan. It follows logically that in such a world there is one, single guide for human conduct.

QUESTION 2 — What are the practical differences between a belief in one G-D and a belief in many gods?

Some of the most basic answers to this question will be developed in the material which follows and in the next lesson. Two or more gods cannot be omnipotent, all powerful. Each must necessarily be limited by the power and activity of the other. But Judaism which stresses *Hashem Echad* encounters no such problem. There is no limit to G-D's power or the range of His activity. A second axiom which results from our belief in G-D's unity serves as the Rambam's third principle. One G-D can be incorporeal, i.e. without a physical body or substance. However, two or more gods must of necessity have limits separating them, limits which belong

to the world of physical substances. It therefore follows that
the concept of *Hashem Echad* is a necessary condition for
the basic Jewish belief that G-D has no physical form and
is not subject to the limitations and weaknesses inherent in
physical bodies. This principle is summed up perfectly in the
third of the *Ani Maamins*:

‏"אני מאמין באמונה שלמה שהבורא יתברך שמו אינו גוף ולא ישיגוהו
משיגי הגוף ואין לו שום דמיון כלל"

"I firmly believe that the Creator is not a body, and that
He is free from all the accidents which plague the body, and
that there exists nothing whatever that resembles Him."

QUESTION 3 — In view of this principle how can we understand the following *posuk* (*Bereshit* 1:27) describing the
creation of man?

‏"ויברך אלקים את האדם בצלמו בצלם אלקים ברא אותו"

Since *Zelem* is usually translated as [G-D's] image, doesn't
this sentence suggest that G-D has a material form?

This question which is often asked is based upon an incorrect definition of the world *zelem*. The Rambam explains
that *zelem* is used to express the essence of a particular thing,
rather than to describe its physical form. The essence of man,
his intellectual, rational ability which differentiates him from
the remainder of creation, corresponds to the *zelem Elokim*.
This is what this *posuk* teaches us; in no way does it suggest
that man's physical form which he shares with the rest of
creation corresponds to G-D.

LESSON 14

IDOL WORSHIP TODAY

In this lesson we shall develop further the concept of *Hashem Echad* with emphasis on its practical implications. In a polytheistic religion which accepts more than one god, the several gods are thought to perform different tasks and to control different spheres of natural and human behavior. Different nations are thought to be governed by different gods. How different is Judaism with its stress on one G-D harmonizing and unifying the whole of His creation.

QUESTION 1 — *Shalom*, peace, is one of the great goals which Judaism strives for. We conclude many of our *tefillot*, e.g., *Shmoneh Esreh, Birkat Hamazon* with a petition to G-D to bring peace to Israel and all mankind. Do you recognize how monotheism makes possible the theme of peace among all the nations? Conversely, do you see how polytheism tends to promote friction and conflict among people of different nations and different cultures?

Hashem Echad, and its corollary, the incorporeality of G-D explains the first two of the *aseret hadibrot*.

„אנכי ה׳ אלקיך אשר הוצאתיך מארץ מצרים מבית עבדים. לא יהיה
לך אלקים אחרים על פני. לא תעשה לך פסל וכל תמונה...״

"I am the Lord your G-D, who brought you out of the land

of Egypt, out of the house of slavery. You shall have no
other gods beside me. You shall not make yourself any idols
. . ." On its simplest level the prohibition against the making of idols and other images brings man closer to a true conception of the incorporeal G-D. But there is a far more profound meaning to this prohibition, with far more relevance
to our contemporary age.

QUESTION 2 — Are many intelligent people today tempted
to place their faith and trust in idols? Has not contemporary
man's sophistication rendered obsolete the prohibition against
idol worship? Do we not all recognize the contrast between
an impotent, powerless idol and the power of G-D, expressed
so beautifully in Chapter 115 of Tehillim which we recite as
the third chapter of *Hallel?*

The first thing we must realize is that no part of Torah
can ever become obsolete due to the passage of time. This
theme will be developed and analyzed in a future lesson; for
the present we need only recognize that since G-D, the
source of Torah, is unchanging, and since the Torah was
meant to be *chukat olam*, its precepts are eternally relevant.
The fact that mankind does change, that with the passage of
time man changes culturally, in no way contradicts the basic
principle. The command: "You shall have no other gods
beside Me" is as relevant today as it was on the day of revelation at Mount Sinai. The idols which man worships today,
although more sophisticated than the stone and wood carvings worshipped in antiquity, constitute false gods just as
much as those statues.

QUESTION 3 — Specifically, what does the prohibition
against idol worship mean to us today? What is the *avodat
zara* of our age?

When an individual places his faith and trust in a man-made idea rather than in the words of G-D, he has made an idol of that idea. There are those who look solely to science for the solution to the problems which we face; others turn for their solutions to various political movements. Absolute faith in science or the various "isms" is a sophisticated form of idol worship, but it remains idol worship. This is not meant to suggest that there is no room for science in Judaism's scheme of things. That is clearly incorrect. However, the proper sense of priorities must be maintained. The word of G-D, the Torah, must be paramount. Science must not become an end in itself, an object of worship. Instead it should be used as a tool to reveal the vastness of G-D's creation.

Nor should we minimize this role. Besides the obvious benefits to all mankind which result from great medical advances, the achievements of modern science have enabled us to have a greater appreciation of the unity of creation. For thousands of years man has attempted to identify the unifying elements which are the building blocks of the universe. The ancient Greeks isolated four elements, earth, water, air and fire. Modern science has shown that the whole world is composed of atoms, and that these atoms are essentially uniform. The different elements which are made up of atoms owe their uniqueness not to any difference in the atoms, but solely to the number of atoms in any particular element.

Question 4 — Until recently science differentiated between two natural phenomena, namely, matter and energy. Do you know how modern physics explains these dissimilar phenomena? What relevance does this have to the unity of the structure of the universe?

Question 5 — In view of the fact that the incorporeality of G-D is a basic belief of Judaism, how can we understand the following Biblical verses?

(שמות ט':ג') „הנה יד ה' הויה במקנך אשר בשדה...".

(שמות ל"א:י"ח) „ויתן אל משה ככלותו לדבר אתו בהר סיני שני לחות
העדות כתבים באצבע אלקים".

(ישעיה א':כ"א) „...עיני ה' המה משוטטים בכל הארץ".

(זכריה ד':י') „...עיני ה' המה משוטטים בכל הארץ".

In each of these sentences, physical organs, e.g., eyes, hands, mouth are ascribed to G-d. These *posukim* are only a sample of similar sentences throughout the Bible which contain anthropomorphisms, i.e., ascribing to G-D physical, human qualities.

The Rambam in his "Guide to the Perplexed" based on the Talmud explains the occurrence of these anthropomorphisms. The Torah wishes to make itself understood. Therefore, *Dibra Torah b'lashon bnei adam.* "The Torah speaks in the language of man." In other words the use in the Torah of human physical qualities to describe G-D is not an accurate representation of G-D. But the Torah uses words from the physical world to describe G-D's nature because only such words are meaningful to us. Man acquires knowledge through the perception of his senses, notably hearing and seeing. When, therefore, the Torah wishes to teach us that G-D has knowledge, it represents Him to us as having seen or heard. Similarly, man communicates his knowledge by speaking; therefore, when the Torah wishes to inform us that G-D has communicated with the prophets, it describes G-D as having spoken with them.

LESSON 15

THE UNIVERSALISM OF JUDAISM

Since we believe that the world and all it contains is the product of one creator, it naturally follows that He is the G-D not only of Israel but of all mankind. This is the universalism of Judaism; G-D is the creator and benefactor of the whole universe. He has established rules of behavior for all men. His *chessed* extends to all, regardless of their nationality or religion. If their conduct conforms to the divine plan, they too are deservant of reward both in this world and in *olam haba*, the world to come. Beside the general relationship between the Creator and all of His creation, G-D has established a unique, special relationship with *klal yisroel*. This unique relationship carries with it added duties and responsibilities, along with the opportunity for added reward. In future lessons we shall explore this unique covenantal relationship with Israel, the *am hanivchar*, the chosen people. In this lesson we are concerned with the universal aspect, the relation of G-d to all mankind, and the response of mankind to that relationship.

That Judaism is a universal religion rather than just one nation's religion can be made clear by the following questions.

QUESTION 1 — Are the first eleven chapters of the Torah
in any way specifically concerned with Jewish history, or with
the history of all mankind? If the Torah did not wish to
stress the universal, would it have bothered to mention the
names of the ten generations between Adam and Noah, and
the ten generations between Noah and Abraham?

QUESTION 2 — According to the Torah, with whom did
G-D enter into the first *brit* or covenant? What are the
essential features of that covenant? Upon whom are the
precepts contained in that covenant binding?

The first covenant between G-D and man is the *brit*
with Noah and his children, after their salvation from the
flood.

(בראשית ט׳: ח׳—ט׳) „ויאמר אלקים אל נח ואל בניו אתו לאמר ואני הנני
מקים את בריתי אתכם ואת זרעכם אחריכם"

"And G-D said to Noah and to his sons with him as follows.
And I establish my covenant with you and with your descendants after you." This covenant with Noah applies to all
mankind for all mankind are descended from him. It establishes seven precepts known as the *sheva mitzvot bnei Noach*
which in their totality comprise an acceptable minimum
standard for man's religious, ethical and legal behavior. The
Talmud (*Sanhedrin* 56b, 57a) lists them: 1) *avoda zara* —
idolatry, 2) *birkat Hashem* — blasphemy, 3) *shfichat damim*
— murder, 4) *giluy arayot* — adultery and incest, 5) *gezel*
— robbery, 6) *dinim* — establishment of courts which enforce
the other six commandments, 7) *ever min hachay* — eating
flesh cut from a living animal.

A gentile who fulfills these seven *mitzvot* is called one of
the *chasidei umot haolam*, "pious of the world's peoples."
Such a non-Jew, although he never embraces Judaism, is

deservant of life in *olam haba.* Maimonides (*Teshuva* 3:5) based on a Mishna so rules:

„וכן חסידי אומות העולם יש להם חלק לעולם הבא"

In future lessons we shall examine the concept of the "world to come." For the present it is sufficient if we realize that eternal life awaits the pious non-Jew as well as the pious Jew.

QUESTION 3 — Does any other religion hold out the promise of eternal salvation to pious people who are not members of that faith? Is this not one further indication of the universal character of *Yahadut?*

The Torah also carefully specifies the treatment which the non-Jew who lives among Jews in a Jewish state can expect. A recurrent theme of the Torah is that Israel should recall its suffering in the days of exile in Egypt as a means of insuring fair and righteous treatment of any non-Jews in the Jewish state. The contrast between the persecution suffered by Jews throughout the long *galut* and the treatment which the Torah requires of the gentile *ger toshav* is striking.

(ויקרא כ"ה : ל"ה) „וכי ימוך אחיך ומטה ידו עמך והחזקת בו גר ותושב
וחי עמך".

"And if your brother became poor and fell into decay, you shall help him although he is a stranger or a visitor so that he may live with you." This *posuk* reflects the true application of brotherhood; the *ger toshav* is called *achicha.* The Jew is required to extend a helping hand at the first sign that the *ger toshav* is in need of aid.

QUESTION 4 — What is the difference between *ger tzedek* and *ger toshav?*

LESSON 16

GERUT: CONVERSION

In the last lesson we saw the effect of Judaism's universalism on the relationship between the Jew and the *ger toshav*, the righteous gentile. The great contrast between the persecution suffered by Jews in most foreign lands and the treatment enjoyed by the *ger toshav* in Eretz Yisroel reflects this principle. We need only contrast the terrible plight and barbaric treatment of our brethren in Arab lands during the past decade with the humane treatment of Arabs in Israel to recognize that this contrast continues into our own day.

The universalism of Judaism also leads to another important distinction between Judaism and other religions, particularly Christianity. Anyone even vaguely familiar with Jewish history both past and present is aware of the forced conversions, often with death as the only alternative, which Christianity attempted to force upon Jews. How different is the approach of Judaism. Not only does *Yahadut* not actively attempt to convert gentiles, but also creates difficulties and roadblocks in the face of the prospective *ger*. In this manner the sincerity of the *ger* can be insured and a conversion merely for convenience sake can be ruled out.

Question 1 — Some of the great figures of Jewish history have been *gerei tzedek.* How many of them can you identify?

Question 2 — Do you understand how the universalism of Judaism discussed in the last lesson is an important factor in shaping the traditional Jewish approach to conversion? Conversely, do you see how the narrow, parochial view of other religions toward people who are not of their faith, has fashioned their approach to conversion?

Question 3 — What are the conditions which halacha requires for a valid *gerut?*

The halacha of *gerut* is designed to promote genuine, sincere conversion and to disallow conversion for insincere or extraneous reasons. It is predicated on one major premise, acceptance of the Jewish religion, *kabbalat ol malchut shamayim.* Jewish nationalism without the Jewish religion is a sham. Let us examine how halacha accomplishes this purpose. The Talmud rules that when a prospective *ger* comes to convert, he is given the following warning.

„גר שבא להתגייר בזמן הזה אומרים לו מה ראית שבאת להתגייר אי אתה
יודע שישראל בזמן הזה דווים דחופים סחופים ומטורפין ויסורין באין עליהם"

"If a *ger* comes to convert, he is told, what 'prompted you to convert? Don't you know that Israel today are broken, thrust down, despised and persecuted?' "

If the prospective *ger* indicates his desire to convert in spite of the above warning, the Beth Din then teach him the essential principles of Judaism. The Gemara specifies that the *ikkarim* of *achdut Ha-shem* and the prohibition against *avoda zara* must be stressed. Certain mitzvot are also taught with stress upon both the potential reward and punishment which depend upon observance. If after the period of study, the *ger* is determined to accept completely and without reservation G-D's Torah, he is ready for the final two indispensable steps which complete the *gerut*. Just as G-D's covenant with *klal yisroel* was sealed by *brit milah* — prior to the exodus from Egypt — and *tevilla* — ritual immersion — prior to *mattan Torah* at Sinai, so too the *ger's* conversion is not valid until *milah* and *tevilla* are performed. *Milah* besides its spiritual meaning of the perfection of the body according to G-D's law, has an important biological factor—it serves as a physical sign of identity with Judaism. *Tevilla* also plays an important symbolic role appropriate for *gerut* since it is a traditional symbol of sanctification and purification. Through the process of *tevilla* the *ger* emerges as a new person—*k'katon shenolad dami.*

QUESTION 4 — What is the status of a *ger tzedek* as compared with a person born a Jew? Is the *ger* in any way a second-class citizen?

LESSON 17

THE EVED IVRI

Throughout the Torah great stress is placed upon the inherent dignity and worth of each human being. The fact that all men were created *b'zelem Elokim*, in G-D's image, is obviously responsible for such a concept of human dignity. In fact Chazal say that every individual should say to himself:

„כל אחד ואחד חייב לומר בשבילי נברא העולם"

"Each individual must say it is for my sake that the world was created." In future lessons we shall see that acceptance of the mitzvot thereby acknowledging G-D as one's master serves a double function: it frees man from the potential tyranny of his own desire (*yetzer hara*) and it frees man from the potential tyranny of his fellow man by establishing G-D as the sole master.

QUESTION 1 — How can we reconcile the institution of *Avdut* sanctioned in the Torah with these two fundamental principles of Judaism? How can we claim that *Yahadut* stresses the dignity and worth of each individual and strives to achieve true human freedom if at the same time it allows one man to be the *eved* of another?

The questions posed here have probably bothered each of us in some form when we first studied *Mishpotim*. However, a great part of the problem can be attributed to faulty definition. *Avdut* is usually defined as slavery, *eved* as slave. It is natural that we identify our understanding of the *avdut* allowed by the Torah with the slavery with which we are acquainted. The sort of slavery which prevailed in the South prior to the Civil War and in the Nazi concentration camps. We shall soon see that this type of slavery and *avdut* are entirely different.

The Torah distinguishes between two types of *avadim*, the *eved ivri* (Jewish) and the *eved canaani* (non-Jewish). We shall discuss each of these types in turn, beginning in this lesson with the *eved ivri*. Halacha recognizes two ways in which a Jew becomes an *eved*. First, he can be sold by the *beth din* in order to repay a person from whom he stole.

QUESTION 2 — All legal systems until very recent times had debtor's prisons where people who could not pay their debts of whatever kind were sent. In fact today even in the United States people are sent to prison for non-payment of certain debts. Did halacha ever allow a person to be sold as an *eved* for non-payment of an ordinary debt? Is not the Torah system whereby a thief makes good his debt to the person from whom he stole, far more constructive both from the point of view of the thief and the person who was robbed, than the system of imprisonment found in all modern countries today?

The second method whereby a Jew could become an *eved* was through a voluntary sale. The halacha here is very clear. A person cannot voluntarily become an *eved ivri* unless he is absolutely destitute and cannot afford the necessities of life.

The following ruling of the Rambam very clearly indi-

LESSON 18

THE EVED CANAANI

In the preceeding lesson we examined the situation of
the *eved ivri*. We found that his position was far more similar to that of a respected employee than to that of a slave.
His *adon* was responsible for his necessities, for the support
of his family, and for luxuries commensurate with the *adon's*
own standard of living.

To a great extent the same principles apply to the situation of an *eved canaani*. The Rambam based on the Talmud,
in both the *Mishna Torah* and the *Moreh Nevuchim*, cautions
the *adon* to treat his *eved canaani* with mercy and kindness.
He is to make certain that the work assigned to the *eved* is
reasonable and within the *eved's* capacity. Again the *adon*
is to feed and provide drink to the *eved*, i.e., necessities of
the same type to which he himself is accustomed. Moreover,
the Rambam, based on the sentence from *Keriyat Shema*:

"ונתתי עשב בשדך לבהמתך ואכלת ושבעת„

rules that just as a person must first feed his animals before
he himself eats, he must also first provide food to his *eved
canaani*.

Question 1 — In societies, both ancient and modern, in which the institution of slavery was practiced, one of the most serious problems is that of physical punishment and beatings inflicted by the master on his slave. Do you recall from your study of Chumash the safeguards established by the Torah to prevent such an occurrence to the *eved canaani?*

Two verses in *Devarim* indicate the length which Torah goes to insure the well being of the *eved canaani.*

(דברים כ״ג : ט״ו) „לא תסגיר עבד אל אדוניו אשר ינצל אליך מעם אדוניו"

"Thou shall not deliver to the master an *eved* who has escaped to you from his master." The Talmud teaches us that this sentence refers to an *eved canaani* who has escaped to Eretz Yisroel. By the operation of this law, the Torah provides the *eved* with an outlet to escape from an oppressive master. Maimonides, in the *Moreh Nevuchim,* derives from here an extremely important ethical lesson which has general and broad implications far beyond the case of an escaping *eved.* "We must always practice the virtue of helping and protecting those who seek our help and not deliver them unto those from whom they flee. And it is not sufficient to give assistance to those who are in need of our help; we must look after their interests, be kind to them, and not hurt their feelings with words. Thus the Torah says:

„עמך ישב בקרבך במקום אשר יבחר באחד שעריך בטוב לו לא תוננו"

Question 2 — Can you translate this sentence? Since it specifically refers to an *eved canaani,* how does the Rambam generalize it to apply to all people who seek our help?

There is one further feature which is essential for the understanding of the institution of *eved canaani,* but which is nevertheless often overlooked. When an *eved canaani* comes into the possession of his Jewish *adon,* he undergoes both *milah* and *tevilla* and pledges to accept those mitzvot which apply to him. In other words during the period of his service to his *adon*, his status differs greatly from that of a slave. It is a period during which he prepares himself for complete *gerut*. While an *eved* he has an opportunity to study the essentials of Judaism under the tutelage of his *adon*. Once he gains his freedom and is willing to accept all the mitzvot, the *eved* becomes a *ger tzedek*, a full-fledged Jew.

Question 3 — What effect does this quasi *rebbe-talmid* relationship have on the *adon-eved* relationship?

Question 4 — Which mitzvot apply to the *eved canaani* and which do not? Can you think of any reason why he is not required to perform all the mitzvot?

Question 5 — Throughout these two lessons *eved* has never been defined as slave. Do you realize why? List the differences in status and treatment between that of a slave as it is commonly understood, and both the *eved ivri* and *eved canaani*.

LESSON 19

AM HANIVCHAR: THE COVENANT WITH ISRAEL

We have already mentioned the divine covenant with Noah and thereby with all mankind. The specific features of that covenant, i.e., the *shiva mitzvot bnei Noach* are appropriate and necessary for all mankind and form an acceptable norm for human behavior. But beyond that covenant with mankind as a whole, G-D formed a unique relationship with *klal Yisroel*. By the terms of this *brit* Israel was selected to serve as G-D's instrument in forming mankind's religious and ethical development. It is for this reason that Israel is known as the *am hanivchar*, the chosen people.

QUESTION 1 – The claim of any nation that it is G-D's chosen people sounds presumptuous, at least to the modern mind. In fact a phenomenon of recent Jewish history has been the attempt by Jewish apologists to play down the concept of *am hanivchar* and to stress only the universalism of Judaism. In order to evaluate this concept, you should consider carefully the following questions. Does history throughout the ages bear out the claim that there is something unique about the Jewish people? Is our history sufficiently different from that of other nations to justify the conclusion that we are an *am hanivchar?* Would you agree that much of the world's history either revolves about the Jewish nation collectively or has individual Jews playing a central role? Of course consideration of this last question should not be confined solely to political events but should include the great intellectual and ethical contributions which have formed modern civilization.

In order to properly approach these questions several things should be kept in mind. First, the selection of Israel as a chosen people gives us rights but also carries with it heavy duties. National calamities are as much a part of *am hanivchar* as are national triumphs. Second, at no time in world history has the number of Jews ever been particularly large. Jews presently comprise between one and two percent of the world's population; it is probable that throughout history Jewish population never greatly exceeded that figure. In fact, the Torah in *Devarim* (7:7) indicates that even in Biblical times Israel was small in number.

„לא מרבכם מכל העמים חשק ה׳ בכם ויבחר בכם כי אתם המעט מכל
העמים"

"G-D did not desire you nor choose you because you were more numerous than other peoples, for you were the fewest of all the peoples."

No attempt will be made at this point to examine in any detail the uniqueness of Jewish history, other than to focus attention on the very fact of Jewish existence. This existence defies all normal historic patterns and is certainly one of the most impressive proofs for the concept of the chosen people. Virtually no trace remains of any of the people extant during the Biblical era. The Egypt of today has nothing in common with Biblical Egypt other than the accident of common territorial location. The language, religion, culture etc., are totally different. But the Israel of today and that of Joshua's

day more than three thousand years ago share many common characteristics. Besides a common language, the observant Jew of today shares with his great-grandfather a common commitment to the Torah. He performs the same
mitzvot, studies the same Torah, follows the same heritage.
This continuity is even more remarkable once we consider
that for the past two thousand years Jews have lived in
exile throughout the four corners of the earth. Certainly
this continued existence is confirmation of G-D's promise to
our *avot* of the eternal character of the Jewish people.

QUESTION 2 — How can we account for the selection of
Israel as G-D's chosen people? Was it an accident, a purely
random selection?

Maimonides, in order to answer this question, analyzes
the history of the period immediately following the flood. All
the sons of Noach believed in one G-D, but thereafter there
began a gradual decline in man's allegiance to G-D. At first
the moon and stars were worshipped not in their own right
but as agents of the one, true G-D. In time the concept of
monotheism was forgotten and every force in nature was
worshipped as if it had its own deity.

QUESTION 3 — The Torah describes this process in the
story of the Tower of Babel. What was the great sin of that
generation as described in the following sentence in *Bereshit*
(11:4)?

"ויאמרו הבה נבנה לנו עיר ומגדל וראשו בשמים ונעשה לנו שם"

QUESTION 4 — How can we account for the fact that the
Babylonians and other ancient peoples have left legends
which in many respects are similar to the Biblical account of
the flood and the story of the Tower of Babel?

LESSON 20

AM HANIVCHAR (Part 2)

The situation prevailing after the *dor haflaga,* the generation dispersed throughout the face of the earth as a result of their rebellion in the Tower of Babel, was not conducive to either moral, ethical or righteous behavior. Man appeared to be repeating the history of the generations prior to Noach which culminated in the flood and the destruction of the greater part of mankind. At this perilous point in the world's history, among the idol worshippers of Casdim, Avraham *Aveinu* was born. Even as a youth he recognized the falsity implicit in idol worship. Without the aid of either tradition or teachers, with only his own reasoning power as a guide, he discovered the truth of *Achdut Hashem.* He broke away from idol worship and turned to the service of the one and only G-D whom he recognized as the creator of heaven and earth. In the face of great opposition and persecution, he dedicated his life to the spreading of *shem Hashem,* successfully gaining many followers.

QUESTION 1 — What became of these righteous followers and disciples? Why were their descendants not chosen as G-D's people?

Thus, the Rambam stresses, it was not by chance that G-D chose Abraham to be the father of His chosen people. He was the one man who by his own intellectual greatness and spiritual grandeur found the way from idolatry to the worship of G-D. G-D does not make a covenant with every righteous man. It is only upon such an extraordinary person as Abraham that G-D will bestow the glory of fathering an *am hanivchar*.

QUESTION 2 — We can now understand why G-D chose to enter into a brit with *Avraham*. However, why should his descendants until the end of time be likewise chosen?

There are several answers to this question. First, the Talmud indicates (*Megilla* 13b) that when G-D selects an individual for greatness as an added reward the greatness is bestowed on his descendants. This explains why the descendants of Aaron continued as Cohanim, and the children of David continued the royal line. There is however an important proviso. These descendants in their own right must merit the position. This leads us to the second answer to our question. The Torah expresses G-D's confidence that Avraham's children would keep the *derech Hashem*.

(בראשית י״ח:י״ט) „כי ידעתיו למען אשר יצוה את בניו ואת ביתו אחריו
ושמרו דרך ה׳ לעשות צדקה ומשפט...".

"For I know him that he will command his children and his household after him, and they shall keep G-D's way to do righteousness and justice." This explains many of the incidents which occurred in the lives of our *avot*. *Akedat* Yitzchak where Isaac without hesitation or hint of rebellion was ready to submit to the *akeda* reinforces the total submission to G-D's will which Isaac inherited from his father. The Torah spells out in precise detail many such incidents in the lives of our *avot* not only because of their historical interest but because these incidents shaped and formed the character of the Jewish people for eternity.

QUESTION 3 — We have so far examined that given the fact of a chosen people, it is proper that Abraham and his descendants should be chosen. But why did G-D wish to establish a unique covenant with a certain people? Just as the covenant with Noah applied to all mankind, why did G-D not see fit to have the Torah apply universally rather than only to Israel?

Just as individuals are not the same, so too the collective characteristics of nations are dissimilar. G-D entered into a limited, uniform covenant with Noah and his sons because G-D foresaw that eventually mankind would divide into different nations with individual characteristics. That is why the covenant with Noah contained only laws which apply universally regardless of the individual peculiarities of the nations. He kept His Torah for that time when there would appear a people whose heritage and training would make them fitting to receive the Torah. The self-discipline and total submission to G-D's will required by the Torah cannot be expected from all peoples. Only *zera Avraham* who inherited from the *avot* the necessary qualities of self-discipline could realistically be expected to carry out the mitzvot.

LESSON 21

THE MISSION OF ISRAEL

In the preceeding lesson we analyzed why *zera Avraham*, the descendants of Abraham, Isaac and Jacob, are a fit people to be chosen as the *am hanivchar*. In this lesson we examine a related topic.

QUESTION 1 — What is G-D's purpose in selecting a particular nation as His chosen people? What is Israel's task in fulfilling its divine mission?

The common goal of all mankind is the Messianic era (which will be studied in detail in a later lesson) described so beautifully in the *al ken nekaveh* with which we conclude each of our daily prayers. We look forward to a time when:

„לתקן עולם במלכות שדי וכל בני בשר יקראו בשמך... ויקבלו כולם את
על מלכותך ותמלוך עליהם מהרה לעולם ועד".

"The world shall be perfect under the reign of the Almighty, and all mankind will call upon Thy name . . . and may they all accept the yoke of Thy kingdom and You shall reign over them speedily and forever." However, mankind must merit the Messianic era; man must reach a certain stage of religious, moral and ethical development before it will be blessed with universal peace and harmony. As the *am hanivchar*, Israel must serve as an example to the rest of mankind, so that they may reach the necessary stage of ethical and religious behavior for the world's redemption.

Question 2 — How does Israel fulfill this task? What unique features make up the role of the *am hanivchar?*

The Torah immediately before the revelation at Mount Sinai which established Israel's selection answers this question.

(שמות י"ט:ה'—ו') "ועתה אם שמוע תשמעו בקולי ושמרתם את בריתי
והייתם לי סגלה מכל העמים כי לי כל הארץ, ואתם תהיו לי ממלכת כהנים
וגוי קדוש"

"Now therefore if you will obey My voice and keep My covenant then you will be to Me a select portion above all nations for all the earth is Mine. And you shall be unto Me a kingdom of leaders and a holy nation." G-D tells us that *am segulah*, the chosen people, involves two interrelated functions. Israel must be both a *mamlechet Cohanim* and a *goy kadosh*. In order to fulfill the function of *mamlechet Cohanim*, — a kingdom of leaders — Israel must first be a *goy kadosh*.

Question 3 — What does *goy kadosh* entail? What is the true meaning of *kadosh?*

Kadosh is usually translated as "holy." But *Kadosh* is really made up of two related themes which in their totality comprise the true meaning of the term. First, *kadosh* means to be separate, removed, distinct from. In order to be *goy kadosh*, Israel must be a nation set apart from the other nations with its own unique way of life. If this unique way of life is to qualify as truly *kadosh*, it must be all-encompassing touching upon all aspects of life, both the mundane and the spiritual. The Torah, i.e., the combination of the written and oral Torah, contain the blueprint which must be followed to be *am kodesh*. The second theme inherent in *kadosh* is dedication which leads to perfection. Dedication to Torah both as a result of intensive study and adherence to the mitzvot found in Torah is the only way that the Jew can be elevated to a state of *kedusha*. In later lessons we shall analyze how performance of mitzvot enable the Jew to reach a state of human perfection. Once Israel lives up to the demands required of an *am kadosh*, it can serve as a *mamlechet Cohanim*, the second great role assigned to it by the covenant.

QUESTION 4 — What was the role of the *Cohen* in the life of Israel during the days of the *Bet Hamikdash?* Were *Cohanim* analogous to the priestly class found in other religions who were set aside as a special social class enjoying special privileges of wealth and power?

Just as the individual *Cohen* dedicated himself to G-D's service and to teaching G-D's law, so too the nation of Israel in its collective priestly task of *mamlechet Cohanim* must dedicate itself to spreading the word of G-D. The comment of Rabbi Ovadiah Sefoarno on the sentence (*Shmot* 19:6) quoted above captures perfectly the role of *mamlechet Cohanim*. "And you shall be unto Me a kingdom of priests. You will be My own treasure from among all the peoples in that you will be a kingdom of priests charged with the task to instruct and teach the whole of mankind in order that they may call upon the name of G-D and serve Him with one consent."

QUESTION 5 — Naturally, our daily tefillot stress the unique covenant with Israel. In both the *Shachrit* and *Arvit* services, the blessing immediately preceding *keriyat shema* stresses the concept of *am hanivchar*. Why is this an appropriate place for this *bracha?*

LESSON 22

TEFILLA: PRAYER

A crucial aspect of Israel's mission is to make obvious in our daily activity our firm belief that G-D is totally involved in the affairs of man. Not only the destiny of mankind as a whole, or of nations, but the affairs of each individual human being, his personal happiness and tragedy, his needs and desires, are the immediate concern of G-D.

QUESTION 1 — Although this principle of *hashgacha pratit*, G-D's concern for each individual, is evident throughout each of the twenty-four books of the Bible, some practical means is necessary to impress it continually on the Jew's consciousness. Do you know how this is accomplished?

If any single mitzva serves this function it is the mitzva of *tefilla*, prayer. In these lessons we shall examine some of the more fundamental aspects of Jewish prayer both in terms of its true meaning and its halachic formulation. The Rambam (*Tefilla* 1:1) derives the Biblical obligation for prayer from *avoda*, service, based on the sentence (*Shmot* 23:25): "And you shall serve the Lord, your G-D." Prayer differs from most other mitzvot in that it is purely *avoda shebelev*, service of the heart. Naturally, as we shall see, this has important consequences for the halacha of *tefilla*.

Shmoneh Esreh is the key *tefilla* of all the prayers we recite. In fact the term *tefilla* is used in the Mishna specifically and exclusively for *Shmoneh Esreh*. We will therefore concentrate in these lessons on an analysis of *Shmoneh Esreh*. In order to understand its unique character, it is necessary to analyze the concept of *kavanah*, the essential element in prayer. The Rambam (*Tefilla* 4:15) tells us that "*Tefilla* without *kavanah* is no prayer." The Hebrew word *kavanah* has no one English equivalent. In Halachic literature it usually means intention to perform an act, concentration and attentiveness. The *kavanah* of prayer has all these connotations, but they do not adequately define the term. Maimonides tells us (*Tefilla* 4:16): "What is *kavanah*? One must free his heart from all other thoughts and regard himself as standing in the presence of the *Shechinah*." This is the essential characteristic which distinguishes the *kavanah* of *tefilla* from that found in other mitzvot, and which distinguishes *Shmoneh Esreh* from other prayers. In *Shmoneh Esreh* man must be acutely aware before whom he stands; he must realize that he is in the presence of G-D.

QUESTION 2 — Why is the *Amida* called *Shmoneh Esreh*? How many individual blessings do we find in *Shmoneh Esreh*?

QUESTION 3 — How can insignificant, puny man confront G-D in a dialogue? Isn't it the height of arrogance to approach G-D with our *bakashot*, our selfish petitions for the satisfaction of our needs? If we really felt that when we say *Shmoneh Esreh* we are speaking directly to G-D, would not we recoil in fear of this dialogue?

The halacha does not allow us to become incapacitated and afraid to approach G-D. It does not allow man to remain mute in awe of the splendor of the Creator. The mitzva clearly requires a Jew to pray daily. The Torah tells us to conquer any inhibitions or timidity and compose ourselves in order to speak with the Creator. If G-D tells man to make *bakashot*, then man is not only granted permission to make petitions, but is justified in making them. Naturally, this does not mean that we may approach G-D in our *tefilla* with chutzpa or arrogance. The Talmud severely criticizes a *mithpallel* who approaches *tefilla* with the expectation that his prayer will be answered as a matter of right. Man may not confront G-D with the attitude that his religious devotion compels the Almighty to grant his petition. The Divine response to the individual's prayer is a manifestation of His grace and mercy, rather than payment to discharge a debt.

QUESTION 4 — Why should prayer be required at fixed times, three times daily? Should not each individual's subjective inspiration be the sole factor in determining when he should pray?

Inspiration for the vast majority of men is rare and infrequent. The pace and turbulence of life, particularly modern life, is not conducive to the religious experience. The spark of G-D found in all men, the drive toward the Creator, can easily be sidetracked by the tensions and distractions of life. When the individual Jew is not ready to enter the presence of the *Schechinah*, the halacha motivates him to marshal his strength for the meeting with *Hashem*. The law demands that man pray, now, at this time, G-D desires that he pray; He is waiting. Armed with such knowledge, man is able to break away from the grip of his everyday reality and transcend the distractions and tensions which surround him. In other words if there would be no requirement to pray daily, most men would not pray except in very rare instances of personal trauma. But man depends upon G-D for his continued existence. An individual's good health or prosperity will disappear in a moment without G-D's constant blessing. It is therefore both fitting and necessary that man's prayer should not be left to individual inspiration but should be subject to the law of halacha.

LESSON 23

THE STRUCTURE OF SHMONEH ESREH

QUESTION 1 — What is the significance of our three daily *tefillot?* Why do we ordinarily recite three prayers each day? How can we explain the additional *tefilla, Musaf,* recited on *Shabbat* and *Yom Tov?*

There are several different but complementary answers to these questions. In other words these respective answers are each true, and once understood in their totality, many of the halachic rules concerning *Tefilla* become more meaningful. The Talmud (*Berakot* 26b) cites two opinions to explain the institution of the three *tefillot* by *Anshei Knesset Hagdolah,* the Men of the Great Assembly, some two thousand five hundred years ago. According to one opinion they were instituted to commemorate the *tefillot* recited by our *Avot;* the Gemara based on Biblical verses indicates that Avraham first recited *Shachrit,* Yitzchak *Mincha,* and Yaakov *Maariv.* The second opinion explains that after *Churban Bayit Rishon,* the destruction of the first *Bet Hamikdosh,* the *Anshei Knesset Hagdolah* standardized the *tefillot* to substitute for the daily sacrifices. *Shachrit* was intended to replace *tamid shel shachar,* the regular morning sacrifice, *Mincha* replaces *tamid shel ben haarbaim,* the regular afternoon sacrifice, and *Arvit* replaces certain offerings remaining from the day's *korbonot* which were brought at night. Since additional *korbonot* known as *Musafim* were offered on *Shabbat* and *Yom Tov*, *Anshei Knesset Hagdolah* instituted *Tefillot Musaf* on those days.

There is another explanation which may be advanced for the institution of the three daily prayers. Man is a composite of the *afar haadama*, the dust of the ground representing man's physical part and the *nishmat chayim*, the divine spark of life representing man's spiritual aspect. Rav Yehuda Halevi in the "Kuzari" explains that just as the physical part of man derives its sustenance thrice daily, so too, the spiritual part of man is nourished three times each day. This is just one example of the balance which Judaism strikes between the physical and spiritual aspects of the human situation.

QUESTION 2 — According to the Rambam daily prayer is a mitzva *deoraitha*, a Biblical command. What was the practice of Jews from the days of Moshe to that of *Anshei Knesset Hagdolah*? Is it possible that Jews did not pray each day during that period? If Jews did pray what exactly did *Anshei Knesset Hagdolah* accomplish with their *takana* of *tefilla*?

Maimonides (*Tefilla* 1:3-4) explains that historical reasons caused *Anshei Knesset Hagdolah* to enact their *takana* of *tefilla*. Certainly from the days of Moses each Jew prayed daily to G-D, but there was no standardized text. Each individual was left free to compose his own personal, spontaneous prayer. However, the Rambam explains, as a result of the Babylonian exile of Nebuchadnezzer and the resultant mingling with the Greeks and Persians, many Jews could no longer properly praise and petition G-D in their prayers. When *Anshei Knesset Hagdola* perceived this state of affairs, they composed and standardized the text of *Shmoneh Esreh* so that the *tefillot* recited should be appropriate for the dialogue with G-D. The text they established with one exception is the very text we recite today. This process described by the Rambam illustrates halacha's method of responding pragmatically to changing practical situations.

QUESTION 3 — Who were the *Anshei Knesset Hagdola?* Why have Jews been so careful to preserve the exact text which they established?

The Gemara (*Megilla* 17b) answers this question.

„מאה ועשרים זקנים ובהם כמה נביאים תקנו שמנה עשרה ברכות על הסדר".

"One hundred and twenty elders and among them several prophets, established the order [and text] of *Shmoneh Esreh*." The Rambam identifies *Anshei Knesset Hagdola* as the prophet Ezra and his *Beth Din*. It is no wonder then that Jews throughout the four corners of the world have zealously guarded and cherished the very wording established by Ezra and his *Beth Din*. The *Shmoneh Esreh* and the other blessings established by the *Anshei Knesset Hagdola* are not the product merely of great poets and philosophers. They are the result of *nevuah*, for only through the medium of prophecy can man properly frame his formal communication with G-D. Jews throughout the world, living continents apart for thousands of years, pray with the same basic text. It is obvious that our major prayers and blessings were created by a central, recognized body and then accepted by all Jewry.

QUESTION 4 — What prayers other than *Shmoneh Esreh* were established by *Anshei Knesset Hagdola?*

QUESTION 5 — Are the individual blessings which make up *Shmoneh Esreh* of one type or several types?

The Rambam (*Tefilla* 1:4) explains that *Shmoneh Esreh* is divided into three separate sections, *shevach* (praise), *bakasha* (petition), and *hodaah* (thanksgiving and acknowledgment). The first section, *shevach*, contains three blessings praising G-D; the middle section is made up of thirteen *brachot* asking G-D to satisfy our personal and national needs; the concluding section is a series of three blessings thanking and acknowledging G-D for all that He does. This formula is based upon the Biblical prayer of Moshe which appears at the beginning of *parshat Va'etchanan* (*Devarim* 3:24-25) and which serves as the archetype or model for all *tefilla*.

„ה' אלקים אתה החלות להראות את עבדך את גדלך ואת ידך החזקה אשר
מי אל בשמים ובארץ אשר יעשה כמעשך וכגבורתך. אעברה נא ואראה
את הארץ הטובה אשר בעבר הירדן"

"Lord, G-D, you have shown your servant your greatness and your mighty hand, for what G-d is there in heaven or earth who can do according to your works and might? I pray of you let me pass over and see the good land that is on the other side of the Jordan." Moshe preceded his request of G-D to be allowed to cross into *Eretz Yisroel* with words of praise for G-D's incomparable greatness and might. Thus in our *Tefilla* we begin with praise of G-D's greatness before we proceed to make our petitions and requests.

QUESTION 6 — Is there any halachic significance to the division of these *brachot* into separate categories?

LESSON 24

THE STRUCTURE OF SHMONEH ESREH (Part 2)

QUESTION 1 — In the last lesson we saw that *Shmoneh Esreh* is divided into three sections. Is there a logical reason for this order? Why should *bakasha* (petitions) be preceded by *shevach* (praise) and followed by *hodaah?* What are the basic themes of the *shevach* blessings?

In lesson 22 we saw that the mitzva of prayer causes man to realize his total dependence upon G-d for the satisfaction of human needs. In the *bakasha* section of *Shmoneh Esreh*, the *mithpallel* specifies the most important needs for his continued well-being. However, it would certainly not be proper for man to arise three times daily and read off a list of his needs to G-D and then depart. Furthermore, it would be virtually impossible for such a prayer to be a meaningful religious experience, rather than a mere lip service to the prayer commandment. Before man can open his heart before G-D in a meaningful expression of petition, he must impress upon himself that G-D is the present and continuing master of the universe. The three *brachot* which comprise the first section of *Shmoneh Esreh* accomplish this purpose by focusing on three separate aspects of G-D's relationships with mankind and Israel. The first *brocha, avot,* deals with G-D's involvement with our forefathers and concludes with an identification of G-D as the protector of Abraham. Its theme concentrates on G-D's role in history, which allowed the people of Israel to flourish and to remain on the world scene despite innumerable attempts to destroy us. Starting with shielding Abraham from the pagans in Ancient Mesopotamia, G-D has continued His special protection to Israel throughout our long history, enabling us to maintain our unique identity. In short, the *bracha* of *Avot* reflects G-D's participation in the historical setting of the Jewish people.

The second blessing known as *gavurot* stresses the Divine presence in the natural world, not only as Creator but as constant sustainer of the natural order. We speak in this *bracha* of G-D as the provider of rain and healer of the sick, but to stress our belief in G-D's control over the forces of nature, we conclude the *bracha* with reference to G-D as reviver of the dead. We, thereby, emphasize our belief that nature's laws are not self-perpetuating. Although G-D has created the universe with an intricate balance of nature, He can alter this balance at will. In the Messianic era one of the most certain of nature's rules will be reversed by G-D and His control over nature will be truly clear.

We conclude the first section of *shevach* by referring to the holiness of G-D in the *bracha* known as *kedushat Hashem*. Not only is G-d master of the world's history and controller of its natural forces, the first two blessings, but also the source of all holiness in the world. It is only after we are aware of these relationships of G-D to the world that we can begin our series of petitions.

QUESTION 2 – Is there any particular significance to the order of the *bakasha* blessings?

There is a definite pattern to the thirteen petitionary blessings which make up the *bakasha* section. The first six

of these *brachot* ask G-D to satisfy requirements of the individual Jew, while the next six refer to the collective needs
of *Am Yisroel*. The thirteenth and final *bracha, Shomea
Tefilla*, sums up this section with a request to G-D to re-
spond to our prayers. In the first *bracha* we ask G-D for
daat, intelligence and knowledge, for this is the distinguishing characteristic of the human being. The next two *brachot*
refer to the individual's spiritual needs. We ask G-D to accept
our *teshuva*, repentance, and grant us *slicha*, forgiveness. We
are then ready to proceed with requests for our material
needs—redemption and protection from enemies, good health
and prosperity.

QUESTION 3 — Why are these *brachot* which deal with the
needs of individuals all framed in the plural form?

The Jew even when he prays for his personal needs does
not selfishly ask only for himself, but rather he requests
G-D's blessing for his neighbors as well. This is not only an
act of thoughtfulness and concern for others, and thereby
an indication of the close bond which unites all Jews, but
also such a procedure provides an important element to
bakasha. It becomes much easier to make personal requests
from G-D if those requests extend to all Jews and not solely
to the individual *mithpallel*. The remaining petitionary blessings call for the reestablishment of Israel in its fullest glory.
They start with a fervent plea for *kibutz galuyot*, the gather-
ing together of all our exiles, and conclude with the ultimate
event, the coming of the Messiah and the restoration of the
Davidic kingdom.

QUESTION 4 — If a *mithpallel* has a specific request which
he would like to incorporate into *Shmoneh Esreh*, is there
any way for him to do so? For example, if a loved one of his
is seriously ill, or if the *mithpallel* faces some other per-

sonal crisis, can the *mithpallel* insert in *Shmoneh Esreh* a specific reference to his situation?

The final section of *Shmoneh Esreh*, *hodaah*, concentrates on thankfulness and acknowledgment. Having completed the petitions, we review the goodness that we have received and graciously acknowledge our total dependence upon G-D. The purpose of concluding with *hodaah* is to impress this realization of total dependence upon the individual, a realization which should be carried over by the *mithpallel* to the everyday, mundane activity which follow prayer.

LESSON 25

DIVINE REVELATION AT SINAI

Certainly the single most momentous and important historical event in the long history of Israel was *Maamad har Sinai*, the Divine Revelation at Sinai. Divine Revelation was the historical event which cemented the earlier covenant with Abraham and made all of Israel know their G-D. G-D, Himself, appeared before the *whole* nation of Israel and it was His voice which spoke the first two commandments, *Anochi* and *Lo yihyeh lecha*. But because of the great fear felt by the people upon hearing G-D's voice, the remaining *dibrot* were spoken by Moshe whose voice was magnified so that it would be audible to the vast throng assembled at the foot of Mount Sinai.

QUESTION 1 — The whole nation of Israel had witnessed with their own eyes many of G-D's miracles, e.g., the plagues in Egypt, the splitting of the Red Sea, the daily *Manna* etc. Is there any difference between the miracles of *Maamad har Sinai* and these other miracles?

QUESTION 2 — Why did G-D feel it necessary to reveal Himself to all of Israel at Sinai? Could He not have transmitted all His law to His people through Moshe without a public revelation?

The Rambam in the *Mishna Torah* explains that the various miracles performed both in the Exodus from Egypt and in the *midbar* were not the decisive factor in Israel's trust of Moshe *Rabbeinu* as G-D's agent. For doubt always is present that events could have been performed as the result of some form of magical power. Furthermore, there was a qualitative difference between the other miracles and Revelation at Sinai. All the other miracles were performed to satisfy a specific physical need of *klal yisroel*, and not as the Rambam says, as a proof of Moshe's prophetic words. But *Maamad har Sinai* was the medium which established firmly *am yisroel's* complete faith and trust in Moshe. *Maamad har Sinai* touched the very spiritual fibre of the people. Objectively, it was not necessary. Certainly, G-D could have dictated the whole of Torah to Moshe Rabbeinu who in turn would have transmitted it to *am yisroel*. But the great spiritual shock produced by the direct hearing of G-D's words instilled deeply into the core of Israel the fear of G-D. The purpose of *gilui Shechinah* at Sinai was to make this *Yirat Hashem* (fear of G-D) a part of the genetic make-up of the Jewish people so that it would be transmitted from parent to child throughout the generations. Furthermore, this faith extended to absolute trust in Moshe and in the words of G-D which Moshe brought Israel. The following *posuk* (*Shmot* 19:9) indicates the second great purpose of *Maamad har Sinai*.

„ויאמר ה׳ אל משה הנה אנכי בא אליך בעב הענן בעבור ישמע העם בדברי
עמך וגם בך יאמינו לעולם...״

"And G-D said to Moses, behold, I come to you in a thick cloud so that the people may hear when I speak with you, and also believe in you forever . . ."

QUESTION 3 — Why did G-D Himself reveal only the first two Commandments and not the whole of Torah at Sinai?

QUESTION 4 — Many religions claim that G-D appeared to one of their prophets and revealed religious truth, or that G-D enabled these prophets to perform miracles. What unique feature of *Maamad har Sinai* differentiates it from the claimed revelation of other religions, and establishes its historical authenticity?

The great difference between *Maamad har Sinai* and the claims put forth by other religions of divine revelation may be found in the fact that *Maamad har Sinai* took place not before one individual, or even a small group, but before the whole nation of Israel. No other religion dares claim a public revelation. In all such claims G-D is supposed to have appeared privately to a single individual. Similarly, no other religion claims that their saints or prophets performed miraculous signs openly before vast throngs. The Resurrection which is the central event in Christian theology is claimed to have been witnessed by only three people.

QUESTION 5 — Do you understand why the public character of *Maamad har Sinai* and the *nissim* associated with the Exodus from Egypt is an excellent guarantee of the historical authenticity of these events? Why does no other religion dare make such claims?

LESSON 26

TORAH MIN HASHAMAYIM: THE TORAH IS DIVINE

In the preceding lesson mention was made of the great psychological shock felt by the people of Israel at *Maamad har Sinai*. We of course cannot begin to imagine how traumatic the experience was. But the Torah both in *Shmot* and *Devorim* describes the fear and trembling which gripped the people. This shock and fear prompted Israel to address the following request to Moshe:

(דברים ה׳:כ״ד) „קרב אתה ושמע כל אשר יאמר ה׳ אלקינו ואת תדבר אלינו את כל אשר ידבר ה׳ אלקינו אליך ושמענו ועשינו"

"You approach and hear all that Hashem our G-D shall say, and then speak to us all that Hashem our G-D shall speak to you, and we will hear it and do it." This request which met with G-D's approval is the basis for the transmission of the Torah by G-D to Moshe, and by Moshe to the people. This is why we call the whole Torah *Torah min hashamayim*, the heaven-given law.

The unquestioned acceptance of the principle of *Torah min hashamayim* is perhaps the single most fundamental belief of Torah Judaism—after the belief in G-D Himself. The Rambam in his formulation of the thirteen principles

93

of faith devotes the eighth principle to this concept. He stresses that the whole of Torah, both the mitzvot and the narrative sections, the legal and historical accounts were dictated by G-D to Moses. Based on the principle of *dibra Torah b'lashon bnei adam*, we say that G-D spoke to Moses but of course the real nature of that communication cannot be really known. It is enough that somehow G-D communicated the Torah to Moses, *word by word* and *letter by letter*, and that Moshe Rabbeinu wrote it down.

Similarly, the Ramban in his Introduction to the Commentary on Chumash stresses this point:

„זה אמת וברור הוא שכל התורה מתחלת ספר בראשית עד 'לעיני כל ישראל' הגיע מפיו של הקב״ה לאזנו של משה."

"This is true and certain, the whole of Torah from the beginning of the Book of *Bereshit* until *'l'enei kol yisroel'* [the last words of *Devarim*] reached the ear of Moses from the mouth of G-D."

QUESTION 1 — Did Moshe write the whole of Torah at one time, or was each *parsha* written immediately after it was dictated by G-D?

The Gemara (*Gittin* 60a) offers two opinions. Rav Shimon ben Lakish based on his interpretation of several Biblical verse says that Moshe actually wrote the Torah at the end of Israel's fortieth year in the wilderness, just before his death. However, the more commonly accepted view is that of Rav Yochanan who is of the opinion that Moshe immediately wrote down each *parsha* after G-D dictated it in separate scrolls. Before his death Moshe combined these scrolls into the very Torah that we have today. The Ramban explains according to this opinion that after Moshe descended from Sinai he wrote *Sefer Bereshit* and most of *Shmot*. Thereafter, each *parsha* was written as it transpired.

QUESTION 2 — The final eight sentences in *Devarim* describe Moshe's death, his burial and Israel's subsequent mourning. Did Moshe also write these *posukim?* If so, is there any difference between the manner in which these sentences were transcribed and the remainder of the Torah?

Once again the Gemara (*Bava Batra* 14b) offers two opinions. According to one opinion, the writing of these eight sentences is credited to Joshua. Rabbi Shimon, however, explains that in fact Moshe wrote the whole of Torah including the account of his death. But there was an important difference. "Up to this point, G-D dictated and Moses repeated it to prevent error and then wrote it down; from this point the last eight sentences G-D dictated, Moses without repeating wrote them with his tears."

QUESTION 3 — Perhaps you know how current halachic practice reflects the different character of the final eight sentences?

QUESTION 4 — What introductory phrase does the Gemara employ to introduce a Biblical quotation? Both the poem *Yigdal* and the *Ani Maamin* which summarize the Rambam's thirteen principles of faith make reference to the principle of *Torah min hashamayim.* Do you understand the following verse from *Yigdal:*

‏„תורת אמת נתן לעמו אל על יד נביאו נאמן ביתו"

The formulation of this principle in the *Ani Maamin* follows:

‏„אני מאמין באמונה שלמה שכל התורה המצויה עתה בידינו היא הנתונה
‏למשה רבינו עליו השלום".

LESSON 27

THE TORAH IS UNCHANGING

QUESTION 1 — What follows necessarily from the fact that the whole Torah is of divine origin?

A necessary corollary to the principle of *Torah min hashamayim* is the firm belief that the Torah will not change and that there will never be another law from G-D. Since G-D who gave the Torah does not change, it follows logically that the Torah which came from Him will not change. Furthermore, since the Torah is G-D's *emet*, it cannot change for divine truth is eternal. Throughout the Torah the term *chukot olam* is employed to teach us of the eternity of Torah. Of course certain conditions which are necessary for the performance of individual mitzvot might not be present, so that those individual mitzvot are suspended. For example, the existence of the Bet Hamikdash is a condition precedent for the application of many mitzvot—until the Messiah comes and the Temple is rebuilt such mitzvot will continue to be suspended. This of course in no way contradicts the basic principle.

QUESTION 2 — The Rambam counts the unchanging character of Torah as the ninth of the fundamental principles of

Judaism. Can you translate its formulation in *Yigdal* and
Ani Maamin?

„לא יחליף האל ולא ימיר דתו לעולמים לזולתו"

„אני מאמין באמונה שלמה שזאת התורה לא תהי' מחלפת ולא תהי'
תורה אחרת מאת הבורא יתברך שמו".

QUESTION 3 — Do you recognize that this principle contains two separate themes? What are they?

QUESTION 4 — How does the principle that the Torah is
unchanging affect the claims of other religions?

Both Christianity and Islam, often called the daughter
religions of Judaism, do not deny that G-D once revealed
Himself to Israel and gave Israel the Torah. In fact both
religions consider the Patriarchs and Moses as prophets of
their own respective religions. Nevertheless, they claim that
a new, *private* revelation occurred which suspended the
original public *Sinaitic Revelation.* However, even a superficial examination of the Torah reveals the lack of basis in
such claims. The Torah specifically rejects the possibility that
anything be either added to or abolished from it.

(דברים י"ג:א') „את כל הדבר אשר אנכי מצוה אתכם אותו תשמרו
לעשות לא תסף עליו ולא תגרע ממנו"

QUESTION 5 — Can you translate this *posuk?* What test
does the Torah advance to determine whether an individual
claiming to be a prophet of G-D is a *navi sheker,* a false
prophet?

The Torah in *Devarim* (13:2-6) immediately after this
posuk indicates that the test of a prophet is not the wondrous
miracles he might be able to perform. For, as the Torah points
out, G-D might see fit to grant unnatural power to one who
comes in the name of G-D as a test of Israel's commitment

to the Torah. A prophet who, speaking in G-D's name, proposes to do away with any of the laws of the Torah, is a false
prophet. Nor should we find this surprising. As has already
been pointed out in a different context, if *klal yisroel* is to
merit the greatest reward, its faith in G-D and His Torah
must prevail over all manner of obstacles to faith.

QUESTION 6 — Do you recognize the contradiction implicit in Christian and Islamic theology?

LESSON 28

TORAH SHE-BEAL PEH: THE ORAL LAW

QUESTION 1 — What is meant by the term *Torah she-beal peh?* Why is it called the oral tradition? What is the source of *Torah she-beal peh?*

In the preceding lesson we examined the divine origin of *Torah she-bektav*, the written Torah. In this lesson we examine the origin and substance of *Torah she-beal peh*, the oral law. This oral Torah is made up of interpretations and amplifications of the written Torah. Much of what we call *Torah she-beal peh* was also communicated by G-D to Moshe at Sinai as a supplement to *Torah she-bektav*. In other words the concept of *Torah min hashamayim* applies with equal force to the oral law. This oral law, however, as its title implies, was not written down by Moshe. Instead it was passed down orally generation to generation in an unbroken chain of continuity until it was finally written down in the Mishna and Gemara. Maimonides in his introduction to the *Mishna Torah* details the outstanding sages in each of the forty generations from Moshe until Rav Ashi who compiled the Gemara. So, for example, Moshe transmitted *Torah she-beal peh* to Joshua, the Elders and the rest of Israel, and from them to the prophets, who in turn transmitted it to *Anshei Knesset Hagdola,* the men of the great assembly, who transmitted it to the Tanaaim. This unbroken chain of tradition is called the *masora.*

QUESTION 2 — How can we be certain of the existence of an oral law of equal divine origin which complements the written Torah? Is there any reference to *Torah she-beal peh* in *Torah she-bektav?*

There are several references in the written Torah to the *Torah she-beal peh.* In *Shmot* (24:12) G-D commands Moshe to go up the mountain and there:

„ואתנה לך את לחת האבן והתורה והמצוה אשר כתב להורותם"

The Gemara (*Berakot* 5a) explains that *"luchot"* refers to the Ten Commandments, *"Torah"* refers to the remainder of Chumosh, *"mizva"* to the Mishna, i.e., the basic principles of the oral law, *"asher kasav"* to the writings of *neviim* and *kesuvim,* i.e., Nach, and *"l'horosam"* refers to the Gemara, i.e., the remaining oral law.

QUESTION 3 — The following posuk in Shmot (34:27) contains a clear distinction between *Torah bektav* and *Torah beal peh.*

„ויאמר ה' אל משה כתב לך את הדברים האלה כי על פי הדברים האלה
כרתי אתך ברית ואת ישראל"

To what does the phrase *"devarim haeleh"* in the first part of the sentence refer? To what does the phrase in the second half of the *posuk* refer?

This *posuk* serves as the basis for an extremely important Talmudic concept; a concept however, which at least at first glance appears to be quite strange and contrary to the commonly understood priorities. The Talmud in Gittin (60b) states:

‫„אמר רב יוחנן לא כרת הקב"ה ברית עם ישראל אלא בשביל דברים‬
‫שבעל פה שנאמר 'כי על פי הדברים האלה כרתי אתך ברית ואת ישראל' ".‬

"Rav Yochanan said that the Holy One, Blessed be He, concluded His covenant with Israel for the sake of *Torah she-beal
peh* alone as it says according to these words [*pi peh*] have
I made a covenant with you and Israel." Similarly, the Talmud Yerushalmi expands this theme and indicates the great
importance attached to *Torah she-beal peh*. "Words [Torah]
were given orally and words were given in writing and we
know not which of the two sets is the more valuable. However, from the verse '*al pi hadvarim haeleh*' we learn that
those that were transmitted orally are the more valuable."

QUESTION 4 — These two selections indicate the great
stress which Judaism places on *Torah she-beal peh*. As you
go through the several lessons devoted to Torah, the following questions should be considered. Why does the Gemara
state that G-D made his *brit* with *klal yisroel* solely for the
sake of *Torah she-beal peh?* Why does the Talmud Yerushalmi state that *Torah she-beal peh* is the more valuable
(*chaviv*)? At the conclusion of these lessons we shall return
to this concept and attempt to place it in its proper perspective.

LESSON 29

TORAH SHE-BEAL PEH (Part 2)

QUESTION 1 — Why is *Torah she-beal peh* necessary? Is not *Torah she-bektav* sufficient?

There are several responses to this question which in their totality form a single basic answer, viz., *Torah she-bektav* without the interpretation and elucidation furnished by *Torah she-beal peh* is often unintelligible or misleading. Let us illustrate this statement with several examples. First, the mitzvot in Chumash are often briefly worded in very general terms. The oral tradition supplies the details necessary for proper observance. For example, in our discussion of *Shabbat* we indicated that *Torah she-beal peh* defines the concept of *melacha*, left undefined in Chumash, to include the thirty-nine categories. Similarly, the mitzva of Tefillin appears in the following cryptic sentence in Devarim (6:8).

"וקשרתם לאות על ידיך והיו לטוטפות בין עיניך"

The Talmud (Sanhedrin 88b) designates Tefillin as a mitzva *deoraitha*, a command which is fundamentally Biblical in essence, but whose *perush*, its interpretation, comes from the oral tradition (*Sopherim*). This means that the primary duty of wearing Telfillin on the arm and on the forehead is ex-

102

plicity found in the Torah, but that the details, such as the actual meaning of the term *totafot*, the passages which are to be selected for placing in the Tefillin, their number etc., are not stated in the *Torah she-bektav*. The Rabbis, however, had received these details by tradition, and have, in addition, found Biblical allusions to them.

QUESTION 2 — Several different approaches within *Torah she-beal peh* are used in its development and formulation of specific Biblical mitzvot. Can you identify some of these categories from your study of the halacha of tefillin? If not, perhaps your teacher would describe these categories using the laws of tefillin as a model.

Torah she-beal peh also fulfills a related but somewhat different function in its explanation of *Torah she-bektav*. Occasionally it modifies the literal meaning of the written Torah. Let us quote what is perhaps the most famous example of this type. In *Shmot* 21:24 the Torah describes the penalty for inflicting physical injury upon the body of a fellow human being.

"עין תחת עין שן תחת שן יד תחת יד רגל תחת רגל"

The Talmud (*Baba Kama* 83b) explains that actually the law does not require the cutting off of the offender's corresponding limb but rather the payment of monetary damages.

QUESTION 3 — Why should *Torah she-bektav* imply that physical payment is demanded from the *mazik*, the one who inflicted the damage, if in reality G-D, as revealed in *Torah she-beal peh*, requires a money payment? Is not such a procedure misleading and isn't it possible that it might lead, *chas vashalom*, to an incorrect understanding of the Torah?

This question is prompted by an implicit assumption which reveals a serious misunderstanding of the relation-

ship between *Torah she-beal peh* and *Torah she-bektav*.
The oral Torah and the written Torah are not two separate
legal systems co-existing one with the other. Rather, they
together make up a single system with a common divine
origin. *Torah she-bektav* without the interpretation of *Torah
she-beal peh* is virtually meaningless. It is only after we recognize this fact that we can properly answer the above question. *Torah she-bektav* says: "An eye for an eye . . . a wound
for a wound" not as a statement of the practical law to be
applied in a given ease, but as G-D's expression of His blame
at one who inflicted injury upon a fellow human-being. It
is as if G-D is saying that the *mazik* deserves to be punished
in kind for the wound he has caused another. Nor is there
any chance of error in applying this law. No serious student
of Torah would ever consider deciding a real legal situation
solely on the basis of *Torah she-bektav*. Reference must
always be made to the *masorah* of the oral tradition.

LESSON 30

THE MITZVA OF LIMUD TORAH

QUESTION 1 — Why was *Torah she-beal peh* originally not written down? In other words why did G-D give part of His Torah in the form of a written Torah, and the remainder in an oral tradition?

The study of any subject requires at the outset a teacher. But after an initial stage of elementary development has been reached, the good student can dispense with a teacher and master his subject through the study of books. But if the particular subject is not put down into writing, a teacher remains an absolute necessity. Torah study is *l'havdil* unlike any other study. For it involves not merely the mastery of an intellectual discipline, but rather a total *derech hachayim*, a detailed blueprint for life. It is obvious that such a study requires a rebbe who not only serves as a source of knowledge, but whose behavior serves as a model to be emulated. By insisting on an oral tradition, the vital talmid-rebbe relationship was insured.

A second answer to this question may be based on the Talmudic statement (*Gittin* 60b) quoted in lesson 28, i.e., G-D made His covenant with Israel solely because of the oral tradition. One of the explanations is that study of an oral Torah is far more difficult than study of a written one since it requires amazing feats of memory.

QUESTION 2 — Why should the difficulty inherent in the study of *Torah she-beal peh* be the reason for G-D's having entered into a covenant with Israel?

Besides the distinction mentioned above between Torah study and all other studies, there is one further crucial difference. Torah study is the performance of a mitzva; it is the single most important service which the Jew can render unto his Creator. This is the meaning of the famous Mishnaic statement (*Peah* 1:1) recited every morning:

„ותלמוד תורה כנגד כולם״

As such the reward which Torah study merits, depends not so much upon achievement as upon effort. Certainly the difference in intellectual ability which exists between individuals should not qualify the brilliant student for a greater reward than the dull student. Rather each individual is judged on how much he has accomplished with his G-D given ability. Since effort is the key factor in the mitzva of *limud* Torah, it stands to reason that *Torah she-beal peh* which requires greater effort is the crucial element in G-D's covenant with Israel.

Let us see how the Rambam (*Talmud Torah* 1:8) formulates the mitzva of *limud* Torah;

„כל איש מישראל חייב בתלמוד תורה בין עני בין עשיר בין שלם בגופו בין בעל יסורין בין בחור בין שהיה זקן גדול שתשש כחו אפילו היה עני המתפרנס מן הצדקה ומחזר על הפתחים ואפילו בעל אשה ובנים חייב לקבוע לו זמן לתלמוד תורה ביום ובלילה שנאמר והגית בו יומם ולילה״

Question 3 — Can you translate this selection? What is the significance of the requirement *likvoa zeman l'talmud Torah?*

Question 4 — The first *parsha* of *keriyat shema* contains the mitzva of *ahavat Hashem,* the love of G-D. Does that *parsha* give any practical advice as to how *ahavat Hashem* may be expressed? In fact unless the Torah gives practical advice on how to express *ahavat Hashem* wouldn't it be a meaningless and virtually impossible mitzva for the great mass of men?

LESSON 31

THE WRITING OF TORAH SHE-BEAL PEH

QUESTION 1 — The Gemara (*Gittin* 60b) based on *Shmot* (34:27) (quoted in lesson 28, question 3) declares that it is forbidden to put into writing *Torah she-beal peh*. In view both of this admonition requiring the oral law to remain unwritten and the advantages of the oral *masorah* with its emphasis on the *rebbe-talmid* relationship, why was *Torah she-beal peh* eventually written down in the Mishna and the Gemara?

In order to understand this process, we must briefly review the Jewish history of the period immediately following the destruction of the Second Temple in 70 C.E. With the destruction of Jerusalem, *churban bayit sheni* and the loss of Jewish political autonomy until our own era, the center of Jewish life moved to Yavneh where Rabbi Yochanan ben Zakkai established a Yeshiva for the continued learning of the Torah. The method of learning called Mishna, essentially involved the systematization of *Torah she-beal peh*, and was carried out by such great Tannaim as Rabbi Akiva and Rabbi Meir.

QUESTION 2 — What does the word *mishna* mean? Why is it an appropriate term to describe the method of study found in Yavneh? Why were the great sages of that period called Tannaim?

However, once Hadrian became the new Roman Emperor in 117 C.E., the situation changed drastically for the worse. He gave orders for the construction of a temple dedicated to the pagan gods of Rome on the site of the ruins of the *Bet Hamikdash* and instituted a series of laws which made it almost impossible to continue Jewish religious and social life. Driven to despair the Jews under Bar Kochba and Rabbi Akiva rose up in revolt in 132. For more than three years Bar Kochba and his followers although greatly outnumbered defeated the best of the Roman legions sent against them. However, the might of Rome eventually prevailed and a period of unprecedented Jewish persecution began. Hadrian correctly realized that Jewish strength and unity was derived from the Torah. He therefore issued a series of edicts designed to destroy both Israel and the Torah. The Yeshiva at Yavneh was closed, the Sanhedrin abolished and an order was issued forbidding on pain of death the study of Torah and the practice of the mitzvot. Many Jews gave their lives rather than comply. Many of those who were not slaughtered or sold as slaves fled to Babylon. But the death of Hadrian in 138 brought some relief and the Yeshivot were reopened principally in Usha under Rabbi Shimon ben Gamliel and his son Rav Yehuda ha-nasi, known in the Talmud as Rebbe.

Rebbe carefully reviewed the situation which his generation faced. He quickly realized that the decimation of the great Sages by the Romans threatened to bring about a situation where *Torah she-beal peh* would be forgotten in Israel. In order to prevent such a calamity, he collected and edited the *Mishnayot*, arranged them systematically in the order which we have today, and [according to the Rambam in the Introduction to his Commentary on the Mishna] actually committed them to writing. According to the Gemara

(*Temurah* 14b), the authority for writing down *Torah she-beal peh* is based on the following drasha.

„עת לעשות לה' הפרו תורתך אמרי מוטב תיעקר אות אחת מן התורה
ואל תשתכח תורה מישראל"

QUESTION 3 — The writing down of *Torah she-beal peh* illustrates the flexibility within the halachic system. In the face of a prohibition to write the oral law, Rebbe, one of the greatest of Chazal, nevertheless did put it into writing. But did he base his authority merely on necessity? Put another way do you understand how this process illustrates the possibility of change, as long as that change is within the framework of halacha? Do you know of other examples of change within the halachic system? Do you agree that a legal system of divine origin, and therefore eternal, necessarily must be flexible to meet changing conditions? But there is an important converse to this principle. Since G-D is the source of the halacha, the basis for any change must be found in halacha. Obviously man has no right to change G-D's law merely for convenience sake or because he does not understand the reason behind a particular halacha.

QUESTION 4 — The *Mishnayot* as arranged by Rebbe are divided into six *sedarim*. These *sedarim* are easily recalled using the mnemonic device *zeman nakot*. Can you identify each of them? Each seder is divided into *massechot* or tractates of which there are sixty-three, and each *massechta* is further divided into *perakim* or chapters. Can you identify at least four *massechot* from each seder? The whole Talmud is often called *Shas*. Do you know the origin of this term?

LESSON 32

THE GEMARA

QUESTION 1 — What are *Baraitot* and *Toseftot?* What is their relationship to the Mishna? What is the Gemara? When was it written?

After the death of Rebbe, life in Eretz Yisroel took a notable turn for the worse. By this time Christianity had been adopted as the official religion of the Roman Empire and an era of Christian persecution of Jews, which was to continue intermittently until our own century, began in earnest. As a result many Jews moved to Babylonia where three major Yeshivot were founded—Sura, under the direction of Rav, Nehardea under Shmuel, and Pumbedita. In these Yeshivot and in those remaining in Eretz Yisroel, the Mishna was diligently studied. The *Amoraiim*, as the sages of this period are called, worked through the Mishna word by word, harmonized apparent contradictions, interpreted its contents and traced back many of these *Torah she-beal peh* teachings to Biblical sources. In situations where differences of opinion existed, the halacha was determined. Moreover, Rebbe in his compilation of the Mishna did not include all the Tannaitic teachings. These were collected and put into writing by Rebbe's contemporaries and his students, notably Rav Chiya, and are called either *Baraita* or *Tosefta*. The

111

Baraitot which often parallel *Mishnayot* are examined in great detail by the *Amoraiim* for any nuances or shades of difference which will cast additional light on the *Mishnayot*. It should be stressed that the *Baraitot* are just as authoritative as the *Mishnayot*. Just as an *Amora* will never contest the teaching of a *Tanna* recorded in a Mishna, unless the *Amora* has a different *Tanna* as support, so too, he will not argue with the teachings of a *Baraita* or *Tosefta* without Tannaitic support.

QUESTION 2 — What is the literal meaning of the terms *Baraita*, *Tosefta* and Gemara? Why are the sages of the Gemara called *Amoraiim*?

The period of *Amoraiim* continued for some two hundred years. Each succeeding generation added new material and interpreted and analyzed the learning of previous generations. Throughout this era this encyclopedia of Jewish learning was not put down into writing. Finally, the great mass of orally transmitted teaching reached such huge proportions that it too required a systematic arrangement and writing down. This great work was undertaken by Rav Ashi who died in 427 and his student Ravina, the last of the *Amoraiim*. Their product was the Gemara which together with the Mishna makes up the Talmud or "study." The Talmud is unlike any other legal compendium in the intellectual history of mankind. Since *Chazal* had such great reverence for the learning of previous sages, the oral tradition was careful to preserve the exact wording and circumstances surrounding the discussions of previous generations. Rav Ashi and Ravina similarly preserved the exact wording of the *Amoraiim* which contributes both to the complexity and unique flavor of the Gemara. It is as if a tape recorder recorded verbatim the discussions of our greatest sages for hundreds of years.

QUESTION 3 — What is the difference between Talmud *Bavli* and Talmud *Yerushalmi?* The relationship between them? Why is Talmud *Yerushalmi* not studied as much as *Bavli?*

Just as Rebbe's Mishna served as the basis for the study in the Babylonian Yeshivot which eventually became Talmud *Bavli*, or the Babylonian Talmud, it also served as the basis of learning in the Yeshivot remaining in Eretz Yisroel. Once again the oral learning was eventually reduced into writing, this time as Talmud *Yerushalmi*. But the respective political conditions of the Babylonian and Israeli communities were significantly different. The Jewish community in Babylonia enjoyed a measure of political autonomy under the *Rish Galuta* or "Prince of Exile," free from persecution and conducive to concentrated study. In fact the Babylonian Yeshivot instituted the *Yarche kalla* ("mouths of the bride," since the Torah is compared to the bride of *am yisroel*) in the months of Adar and Elul which attracted scholars from all walks of life and professions. The conditions in Eretz Yisroel were not nearly as favorable since the Christian persecutions nearly made life unbearable. This explains why Talmud *Yerushalmi* did not become as popular a source of study as *Bavli*. Since it is approximately one third the size of *Bavli*, it is not as complete. Nor is its text as clear and certain. Equally important, the great *Rishonim* such as Rashi and Tosafot whose commentaries often make difficult passages of the *Bavli* intelligible, did not directly write *perushim* on *Yerushalmi*. But this should not lead you to believe that Talmud Yerushalmi is unimportant. Great *talmidei chachamim* during the eras of *Geonim, Rishonim* and continuing to our own day have studied *Yerushalmi* as carefully as *Bavli*. Those of you who have been privileged to study Tosafot probably recall instances where passages from the *Yerushalmi* are quoted and analyzed.

QUESTION 4 — During what periods and where did the *Geonim, Rishonim* and *Achronim* flourish? Who were the *Ashkenazim* and *Sefardim?* Can you identify the outstanding *gedolim* of each of these periods?

LESSON 33

TALMUDIC METHODOLOGY

QUESTION 1 — Why does the Talmud assume that the earlier the era, the more it is authoritative? Why will an *Amora* never argue with a *Tanna*, and a *Rishon* with an *Amora?*

Since *Torah she-beal peh* is an oral tradition, it is obvious that the closer an era is to the source of revelation, the greater the probability that the leading sages and scholars of that era will have a more perfect understanding of all the nuances of Torah. In fact the Rambam in the Introduction to the Commentary on the Mishna teaches that differences of opinion concerning even minor aspects of the *Masorah* did not arise until well into the Tannaitic period. This explains why the Talmud does not associate particular *halachot* with the names of individual sages who lived and taught during the centuries between the age of Moshe and the age of the Tannaim. But just as a person's mind requires a healthy body to function best, so too Israel's intellectual and spiritual achievement reflected changes in its political and social situation. From the time of Moses until the destruction of the first Temple, Israel was an independent nation living together in Eretz Yisroel. It was period of *nevuah*, when prophets came before the people and spoke in the name of

G-D. During the Tannaitic period Israel was no longer free of outside interference and persecution, but at least all the great sages were assembled together in Eretz Yisroel. The epoch of the *Amoraiim* marks a qualitative change—the Roman ravages had taken their toll, most of the great sages were no longer located in Eretz Yisroel, political power was wielded by gentile authorities. Nevertheless, the great scholars were concentrated together and at least in Babylonia some measure of independence and material comfort was retained. The age of the *Rishonim* is substantially different. Persecutions in Babylonia eventually forced the Jewish community to flee and the great sages were scattered throughout Europe and North Africa.

QUESTION 2 — How can we account for the existence of *machlokot*, differences of opinion, among *Chazal?* In which of the categories of *Torah she-beal peh* do we find *machlokot?*

The Rambam (ibid.) distinguishes between four major categories of *Torah she-beal peh.*

1) *Halachot* transmitted to Moshe at Sinai (and thereafter throughout the generations as part of the *masorah*) for which support may be found in *Torah she-bektav.*

2) *Halachot* transmitted at Sinai for which no scriptural support of any kind may be found. These laws are called *halacha l'Moshe mi-Sinai.* The Rambam forcefully makes clear that in each of these categories no *machlokot* are found concerning any matter of fundamental importance.

3) *Halachot* which were transmitted to Moshe at Sinai (and which have been practiced by *klal yisroel* throughout the generations) which can be derived from *Torah she-bektav* either as a result of a logical inference, e.g., *kal v'chomer*, or as a result of the various exegetical methods of *drasha* (the most famous of which are the thirteen *middot* of Rabbi Yishmael recited each morning at the conclusion of

korbonot) e.g., *gezara shava, klal prat klal,* etc. In the next lesson we shall examine in detail the operation and purpose of such *drashot.* For the present we need only mention that in this category we do find *machlokot.* But as the Rambam makes clear these differences of opinion do not question the validity of the specific halacha. Instead the arguments question the applicability or the logic of a particular *drasha* selected to prove from *Torah she-bektav* the halacha.

4) *Gezerot* which were enacted by the prophets or in later generations by the great sages in order to "erect fences around the Torah." (This topic has already been dealt with in lesson 12.) Naturally differences of opinion as to whether a specific piece of Rabbinic legislation was necessary arose and produced the largest amount of *machlakot* found in the Talmud.

LESSON 34

TALMUDIC DRASHOT

QUESTION 1 — How can we account for the many *drashot* found in the Gemara where *halachot* are derived from *Torah she-bektav* through the use of such principles of interpretation as *hekesh, gazara shava, klal prat klal* etc? What is the authority for such *drashot?*

In order to answer this question, we must first consider some facts concerning G-D's creation. The physical world does not contain creations which serve no purpose. Scientists continually find that a particular organ or a natural phenomenon which was thought to be purposeless serves an important function. But the Torah is also G-D's creation. When G-D "created" the Torah, it was with the same precision and care as the rest of creation. Every superfluous word or letter, the usage of identical words or phrases in different passages (for *gezara shava*), the placing together of different subjects in one passage to draw an analogy or *hekesh* were all done purposefully. Similarly, the placement of a word or letter in a particular place for one of the thirteen *middot* enumerated by Rabbi Yishmael follow a divine plan. The general outline of each of the *middot* is part of halacha *l'Moshe mi-Sinai*, in other words the rules of interpretation are also of divine origin. This does not mean that the particular details of all

Talmudic *drashot* are necessarily of divine origin. In fact all *meforshim* agree that a *kal v'chomer* or purely logical inference may be made by *Chazal* on their own without the benefit of *Masorah*. On the other hand all agree with the following statement of Rashi (*Succah* 11b) that not even *Chazal* could make on their own a *gezara shava* without the benefit of *Masorah*.

„אין אדם דן גזרה שוה מעצמו אלא אם כן למדו מרבו ורבו מרבו עד
משה רבינו...".

QUESTION 2 — Since there is unanimity that *"ein adam dan gezara shava meatzmo"* how can we explain the *machlokot* which revolve around a particular *gezra shava*? Similarly, why does the Gemara question the selection of a specific word for the *gezara shava* and suggest another, and why does the Gemara occasionally praise a scholar for suggesting a *gezara shava*?

These questions were raised by the Rambam in his Introduction to the Mishna and by the Ramban in his Commentary on *Sefer Hamitzvot* (*shoresh bet*). Each answers that although *masorah* must point to the existence of a particular *gezara shava*, it need not and often did not supply all the details. It is concerning these details that we often find *machlokot*.

Let us see how *Chazal* use the various exegetical rules in interpreting *Torah she-bektav*. A key principle is contained in the Talmud *Yerushalmi*: "One may apply *gezara shava* to support his teaching, but not to invalidate it." This means that *Chazal* employed these rules *only* for the purpose of giving a scriptural basis to the *halachot* which were already taught and known as part of *Torah she-beal peh*. On the other hand, none of these rules could be used to fashion a *drasha* which would conflict with a halacha which had been transmitted in the *masorah* as part of *Torah she-beal peh*.

QUESTION 3 — Why should *Chazal* feel it necessary to find support in *Torah she-bektav* for the *masorah* of *Torah she-beal peh?* In order to answer this question, you should consider the selections quoted in Lesson 28, question 4, which stressed the importance of *Torah she-beal peh?*

The quotations from *Gittin* (60b) and the Talmud *Yerushalmi* indicate that *Chazal* meant to forcefully convey the importance of *Torah she-beal peh* as the major factor in fashioning the halacha, the *derech hachayim* which G-D demands from each of His people. However, *Torah she-bektav* fulfills a unique function even in the formulation of those *halachot* which are essentially a part of *Torah she-beal peh* because it serves as testimony to the oral tradition. This role of *Torah she-bektav* is made clear in *Devarim* (31:26) where Moshe commands the Levites to place the Sefer Torah in the Holy Ark:

„והיה שם בך לעד"

"It shall be there for you as a witness." Among the several forms of testimony which the written Torah provides is that of *edut* to the truth of the oral tradition. When *Chazal* in the Talmud use *hekesh, gezara shava* or other such *drashot* as support for the *masorah* of *Torah she-beal peh* they are thereby fulfilling the great role of the written Torah as testimony to the truth of the *Masorah*.

QUESTION 4 — Don't *drashot* occasionally appear to be contrary to the literal meaning of the text, for example, sometimes an *Amora* will say "*al tikri*", do not read the text as we have it, and substitute another letter? Is not such a drasha contrary to the accepted principle that the interpretation of the text should not deviate from its *pshat* or literal meaning?

In order to answer this question we must distinguish

between two types of *drashot*. Until now we have discussed the use of scripture as *edut* to the *masorah* transmitted at Sinai. In other words law which has the force of *deoraitha*. But the oral tradition also included a great mass of Rabbinic law and midrashic and aggadic teachings. This material placed a great burden on memory. In order to facilitate this memory *Chazal* found a basis in *pesukim* or verses of the Torah. This form of *drasha* is known as *asmacheta*, or hint. The *pshat*, the literal meaning of the Torah remained intact; the *drasha* was intended as a pedagogical device to make memory easier. This theme will be discussed in greater detail next lesson in connection with aggadic *drashot*.

LESSON 35

THE AGGADA

The Talmud contains far more than halachic material which deals with the practical observance of Jewish law, both religious, criminal and civil. Side by side and often interwoven with the legal discussions is the Aggada or non-legal teaching which covers a wide range of subject matter. In any discussion of Aggada it is essential that the student recognize that the body of teaching is varied in terms of both its source and pedagogical objective.

QUESTION 1 — Can you identify different types of *Aggadot?* What was *Chazal's* objective in their exposition of these respective *Aggadot?*

Certainly the single most important class of Aggada is that which deals with the philosophic foundations of our faith. Since many of the lessons which follow are devoted to an analysis of specific fundamental concepts, no attempt will be made in this lesson at any detailed examination of such *Aggadot*. But one crucial preliminary observation is in order. Just as many basic halachic principles were transmitted orally by G-D to Moses at Sinai and thereafter from generation to generation, so too the basic philosophic principles are part of Torah *min hashamayim*. Once again, *Chazal* used the various exegetical rules, such as *gezara shava* and *hekesh* to deduce support from Torah *she-bektav* for this oral *masorah*. The following quotation from the work of Rabbi Zvi Hirch Chayes who wrote extensively on Talmudic methodology and particularly Aggada clearly indicates the correct approach which we are to take concerning the source of these *Aggadot*. "But one sure fact undoubtedly remains, and that is that all these came down orally from the words of G-D to Moses our teacher; for if concerning the practical observance of the mitzvot and the physical duties required by them, which are but a preliminary to the purity of religious life, they had halachot traditionally received from Sinai, teaching how they were to be applied in various conditions and situations, how infinitely more is this view to be applied to matters of faith and the fundamentals of religion, such as the immortality of the soul and *olam haba* . . ."

QUESTION 2 — Do you recognize the *kal v'chomer* contained in this selection? Can you state it clearly in your own words?

A second category of *aggadot* relates events which occurred in Israel's past, particularly those which revolve about the great figures in Jewish history. Often these *Aggadot* are introduced with the phrase "It is a *masorah*" or "We have it by tradition." These stories are clearly not the *Amoraiim's* fabrication; they are historical occurrences which so impressed the people that they were transmitted from parent to child as part of the oral tradition.

A third class of *Aggadot*, extremely common in the Gemara, requires a fuller discussion. *Chazal's* purpose in these *aggadot* is to impress upon *Am Yisroel* the importance of ethical behavior. In order to underscore the stress Judaism places on virtuous, ethical and moral conduct—in other words on *gemillat chasadim*—and its abhorrence of non-ethical selfish conduct, *Chazal* purposely exaggerated the consequences which follow either type of conduct. In addition to exaggeration, as a further means of impressing upon Israel the importance of *gemillat chasadim*, *Chazal* employed the usual exegetical rules such as *gezara shava* to support their moral teaching from the Bible. Thus, for example, the Gemara (*Ketubot* 68a) says: "Whoever turns his eyes from the practice of charity should be regarded as though he were an idolater [based on a *gezara shava*, the word *bliyaal* appears in two contexts, one *Devarim* (15:9) dealing with the duty of helping the poor and the other *Devarim* (13:4) dealing with the idol worship]." Similarly, *Nedarim* (40a): "He who does not visit the sick is comparable to a murderer." Obviously these maxims are not to be understood literally. But certainly, after seeing the last statement in the Talmud, the ordinary Jew will not belittle the mitzva of *bikur cholim*.

The Talmud also contains certain *Aggadot* which are clearly not to be understood literally but are meant as allegories containing profound secrets. *Chazal* obviously deemed it best that certain matters should be hidden from the ordinary student. The Rashba with reference to an aggadic statement in *Berakot* (6a) makes the following comment: "Note that the *Aggadot* of the Rabbis contain hidden ideas and thoughts merely hinted at, and if these appear as worthless words to the ignorant, to those of understanding who are aquainted with hidden wisdom these words deal with subjects demanding the highest intellect . . . But in no case do such *aggadot* mean merely what the words convey."

The final category of *Aggadot* with which we shall deal concern Talmudic statements concerning medicine, mathematics and assorted scientific subjects. It should be understood that these discussions reflect the most advanced scientific knowledge known in the age of the Talmud. In fact much of the practical advice particularly relating to diet found in the Gemara has been shown to be correct by the latest findings of contemporary science. Nevertheless, it should be realized that this knowledge is not of divine origin, it is not Torah *min hashamayim,* and as such it can be refined and corrected by later more advanced scientific observation.

QUESTION 3 — What are the *Midrashim?* With what does the *Mechilta, Sifri, Sifra* and *Midrash Rabba* deal? When were they written and by whom?

LESSON 36

BECHIRAT CHAFSHIT: FREE-WILL

One of the most significant doctrines of Judaism which makes possible so much of Jewish theology is that of individual *bechirat chafshit* or free-will. The Rambam (*Teshuva* 5:1) begins his discussion of this subject by stating that every man can choose for himself whether to do good or evil. It is this great gift which distinguishes mankind from the remainder of G-D's creation; *bechirat chafshit* is the unique characteristic of man. The following sentence in *Bereshit* (3:22) in reference to the "tree of life" makes this point clear.

„ויאמר ה' אלקים הן האדם היה כאחד ממנו לדעת טוב ורע".

Man is compared to G-D Himself as a result of his ability to choose between *tov* and *ra*. It is not surprising that such a fundamental concept raises important philosophical questions. Let us analyze some of them.

QUESTION 1 — How can man freely choose to do as he pleases? Does not such freedom of choice limit G-D's power?

A little reflection quickly reveals the fallacy behind this question. *Bechirat chafshit* is not an accident of nature. Man's freedom of choice is as much a part of G-D's will, as, for example, the law of gravity. Just as an object falls down rather than up, so too G-D has established man's *bechirat chafshit* as a rule of nature. There is a paradox here; man's freedom from G-D's control in the choice of his actions is itself part of G-D's control, part of the divine ordering of the universe.

QUESTION 2 — If there would be no *bechirat chafshit* would the existence of the Torah, a divine system of law make any sense? In the absence of free-will, would a system of *schar v'onesh*, of reward and punishment, human responsibility for individual actions be possible? Do you recognize why *bechirat chafshit* makes possible these basic principles of Judaism?

QUESTION 3 — Are there not examples in Torah which seem to contradict the principle of *bechirat chafshit*, and imply that G-D controls an individual's choice of doing good or evil? For example, how can we explain the sentence in *Shmot* (7:3):

‏״ואני אקשה את לב פרעה והרביתי את אתתי ואת מופתי בארץ מצרים.״‏

"And I will harden Pharaoh's heart and multiply my signs and my wonders in the land of Egypt"?

Both Rashi in his explanation of this *posuk* and the Rambam grapple with the problem raised by this question, and each reaches a similar conclusion. Occasionally a man's actions are so sinful and abhorrent to the merciful G-D that even *teshuva* cannot undo his fate. Such a man was Pharaoh who was directly responsible for the great suffering in Egypt and who ordered the murder of all the male Jewish infants. Nevertheless, as Rashi points out based on a Midrash, G-D did not "harden his heart" until after the first five plagues. In other words during the first five plagues the choice of

repentance was freely left to Pharaoh. He did not avail himself of the opportunity of acknowledging G-D, which would
have saved him from the consequences of his earlier behavior.
It was only thereafter that G-D "hardened his heart" which,
as the conclusion of the *posuk* indicates, enabled G-D to
multiply his "signs and wonders," so that *Bnei Yisroel*
would recognize Him.

QUESTION 4 — Philosophers throughout the ages and of
all religions have been troubled by a philosophic dilemma.
How can we maintain that man has freedom of choice, when
at the same time G-D has foreknowledge of every human
deed? Since G-D knows what each individual will choose, is
the eventual choice really free?

Rabbi Akiva in *Pirke Avot* (3:15) gives the definitive
Jewish approach to this problem.

"הכל צפוי והרשות נתונה"

"Everything is foreseen [by G-D], yet freedom of choice is
given." The *Rishonim* advance two interpretations by way
of explanation. The Raavad maintains that G-D's prior knowledge in no way determines man's choice. It is as if by way
of analogy someone could look into a crystal ball and see
that I will choose orange juice rather than milk for break-
fast tomorrow morning. In no way is the choice influenced
by what was seen in the crystal ball.

The Rambam offers a different approach. He begins by
distinguishing between human knowledge and G-D's knowledge. Man's self and what he knows are separate and distinct.
But G-D's essence and His knowledge are one and the same.
Just as it is beyond human capacity to discover G-D's true
nature as the Torah says in *Shmot* (32:20): "For man shall
not see [understand] Me and live," so it is beyond human
ability to really comprehend G-D's knowledge. As explained

by later *meforshim*, the Rambam means to teach us that since G-D is outside time He sees events in an eternal present. When a man sees someone else doing something, the fact that he sees it does not necessarily influence the actor. Similarly, when G-d sees a man doing something, He exercises no control for before G-D there is no past or future; He is beyond time.

LESSON 37

OLAM HABA: THE WORLD TO COME

We begin in this lesson an analysis of three related subjects each of which is a fundamental *ikkar* of *Yahadut*, viz., *olam haba* (the world to come), the age of the Messiah and *techiyat hamatim* (the resurrection of the dead). G-D in his infinite wisdom did not in the Torah give a detailed picture of *olam haba*. The Torah as we shall see promises that there is an *olam haba* followed by the physical resurrection of the dead, but no more is revealed. Similarly in *Nach* the prophets deal extensively with *yemot hamashiach* but little is added concerning *olam haba* and *techiyat hamatim*.

QUESTION 1 — How can we explain the lack of detail in the Torah concerning *olam haba* and *techiyat hamatim?* What possible purpose is served by the lack of precise detail concerning such fundamental principles?

In order to answer this question, we must make a brief and preliminary sketch of Judaism's concept of the world to come. According to *Chazal* there are three distinct stages—with the term *olam haba* being applied to both the first and third stages. Upon the death of the body, the individual's soul does not cease to exist. Instead it remains in a purely spiritual state apart from the body and each individual soul enters the heavenly world. The second stage is *yemot hama-*

shiach which is the ideal natural state on this earth. Finally, there is *techiyat hamatim* where the bodies of the dead are reunited with their personal souls in a perfect life. Since the first stage of *olam haba* involves a purely spiritual state, it is impossible for us who live in a corporeal or physical world to comprehend it. Just as a person blind from birth cannot possibly appreciate the spectrum of colors, we of this earth cannot comprehend the pleasures of the spiritual world. This explains why the Torah and the prophets do not attempt to describe the perfect bliss which awaits the righteous in *olam haba*. Such a description is beyond the comprehension of man as long as he lives in the physical world. Furthermore, if anything, such a description would have a negative effect for it would decrease the worth of *olam haba* in our eyes. In fact the Rambam after he describes the spiritual bliss of *olam haba*, recognizes the danger that the description does not appear particularly attractive to many men who conceive of happiness only in physical terms. Let us quote in translation the Rambam's words (*Teshuva* 8:6): "This type of goodness might seem a light matter in your eyes and you may imagine that the only proper reward for keeping G-D's commands and being perfect in the ways of truth is to eat and drink well, . . . to wear choice garments of linen, to live in marble palaces and to use gold and silver utensils, etc. . . . These things are only valuable to us in this world since we have a body and are corporeal and these are bodily wants. The soul desires them only because the body wants them in order to be healthy. But all these have no value when there is no longer a body to enjoy them."

QUESTION 2 — If an infant is offered the choice between a piece of candy and a diamond, which will he select? What about an adult? Do you see the relevance of this question to the preceeding discussion?

The most famous Talmudic statement concerning the first stage of *olam haba* is that of Rav (*Berakot* 17a):

„העולם הבא אין בו לא אכילה ולא שתיה ולא פריה ורביה ולא משא
ומתן לא קנאה ולא שנאה ולא תחרות אלא צדיקים יושבים ועטרותיהם
בראשיהם ונהנים מזיו השכינה."

"In the world to come there is neither eating nor drinking nor reproduction nor business, there is neither jealousy nor hatred and there is no strife. But the righteous sit with their crowns on their heads and enjoy the splendor of the *Shechina*." Maimonides explains (*Teshuva* 8:2) that the reference to the *tzadikim* "sitting" is figurative, i.e., *tzadikim* exist in *olam haba* without toil or effort. The reference to the "crowns" on their heads means that their personal knowledge is with them there and serves as their crown, i.e., glory.

QUESTION 3 — Once we understand the purpose behind the absence of detailed description of *olam haba* in the Torah, one question remains. Are there any sources in Torah and the Prophets which indicates the existence of *olam haba* and the immortality of the soul or is this concept solely a part of Torah *she-beal peh?*

Let us begin with an argument based on logic.

We know from *Bereshit* that man was created from two components, the dust of the earth and the *nishmat chayim*, the divine spark. The Ramban in his commentary on *Chumash* (*Vayikra* 23:29) explains that since man's soul comes from the immortal creator it obviously must be immortal. "The soul of man is the *ner* of G-D which He has breathed into man. It must thus remain in its state and cannot die . . . its continued existence being necessary and enduring forever." In other words, it is inconceivable that a divine object could be subject to death. Furthermore, the Torah clearly indicates that the immortal soul can be held responsible for human sin. In *Bereshit* (9:5) the Torah forbids suicide under the pain of punishment when it says of one who commits suicide: "And surely your blood will I require of your souls." But if death is the end, there would be no possibility of punishment. Similarly, as the Ramban points out, the grave penalty of *karet* (cutting off i.e., no share in *olam haba*), mentioned often in Torah as the punishment for serious offenses against G-D indicates that immortality awaits those who have not sinned.

There are many references in *Tanach* to the immortality of the soul. Let us quote just one representative *posuk* from *Tehillim* (49:16)

„וְאַךְ אֱלֹקִים יִפְדֶּה נַפְשִׁי מִיַּד שְׁאוֹל כִּי יִקָּחֵנִי סֶלָה"

"For G-D will redeem my soul from the abode of the dead, for He shall receive me."

LESSON 38

THE AGE OF THE MESSIAH

The second stage, *yemot hamashiach*, unlike *olam haba* is revealed in detail in both Torah and the Prophets. Accordingly, the Rambam (*Melachim* 12:1 and commentary on Mishna *Sanhedrin* 10:1 twelfth principle) warns that any Jew who entertains any doubt concerning the eventual coming of the Messiah is guilty of denying not only the clear words of *all* the prophets but of the Torah itself.

QUESTION 1 — Where in the Torah can we find assurance concerning the coming of the Messiah?

The Torah in several places testifies to the Messianic era. Moshe, on the day of his death, assembled all Israel whereupon he prophesized that Israel would be dispersed throughout all the lands of the earth for having broken its covenant with G-D. But finally as the *posuk* concludes (*Devarim* 30:3):

„ושב ה' אלקיך את שבותך ורחמך ושב וקבצך מכל העמים אשר הפיצך
ה' אלקים"

"Then the Lord your G-d will turn your captivity and have compassion on you upon you, and will return and gather you from all the peoples where G-D had scattered you."

134

Similarly, in the chapter of Bilaam (*Bamidbar* 24:17-21), the Torah prophesizes the coming of David and at the end of days the *melech hamashiach*. These verses describe the essential characteristics of the Messianic era. The Messiah will lead Israel in the reestablishment of the Davidic dynasty. The Children of Israel exiled throughout the four corners of the earth will return to *Eretz Yisroel*. The *Bet Hamikdash* will be rebuilt and all the mitzvot which depend on the Temple will be reinstituted.

QUESTION 2 — Will *Yemot Hamashiach* affect only Israel or does it extend to all mankind? What will be the relationship between Israel and the other nations at that time?

We have already made reference in a previous lesson to the fact that the Messianic era is the common goal of all mankind. The spiritual and material restoration of Israel will regenerate all mankind who will recognize G-D in the words of Zechariah (14:9) with which we conclude our daily prayers:

„והיה ה' למלך על כל הארץ ביום ההוא יהיה ה' אחד ושמו אחד"

The Rambam quotes approvingly the famous statement of Shmuel (*Sanhedrin* 91b):

„אין בין העולם הזה לימות המשיח אלא שיעבוד גליות בלבד"

"There is no difference between this world and the Messianic era except for subjugation to kingdoms." This refers not only to Israel but to all nations. No nation will fight against another; war, violence and conquest will disappear. Mankind will work together toward the common goal of spiritual and material perfection. This perfection is described by the Rambam in the final halacha of the "Mishna Torah" (*Melachim* 12:5): "In those days there will be neither famine nor war, nor jealousy nor strife, material goods will be in abundance

and luxuries will be as plentiful as the dust." Besides these
blessings enumerated by the Rambam, the prophets include
the healing of the sick and the lengthening of human life.
Along with these material blessings, *Yemot hamashiach* will
be a time of spiritual and moral perfection. Once all mankind
will acknowledge G-D, a new spirit of justice and mercy will
replace the selfishness and cruelty so common today. The
nations will recognize Israel as the source of ethical and
righteous teaching and will seek out Israel as its teacher.
The prophet Isaiah (2:3) has this in mind when he says:

"כי מציון תצא תורה ודבר ה' מירושלים"

"For out of Zion shall go forth the law, and the word of the
Lord from Jerusalem."

QUESTION 3 — Does not the Rambam appear to contradict himself? On the one hand he recounts the great material
and spiritual blessings to be found in *yemot hamashiach,* so
different from the world as we know it, and at the same time
he quotes Shmuel's statement that the only difference between *olam hazeh* and *yemot hamashiach* is *shibud goliyot.*

In truth the Rambam is not guilty of any contradiction
but rather gives us a remarkable insight into the human
situation. Much of the pain and suffering that our world
knows is due to the passions which produce war and strife.
But once man rechannels his energies from war to peace,
from selfishness to justice and mercy, from defying G-D to
acknowledging Him, the great material and spiritual blessings
of *yemot hamashiach* will follow naturally. This is not meant
to suggest that G-D will not perform miracles in *yemot
hamashiach.* All that is meant is that once the *Mashiach* is
sent to us as a leader mankind can reach a state of perfection even without further miracles, not *chas vachallila* to
foreclose G-D's performing additional miracles. In fact the

yemot hamashiach will be climaxed by the great miracle of *techiyat hamatim* to be examined in the next lesson.

QUESTION 4 — Is there any way of calculating when the Messiah will come? Is such speculation proper?

The Talmud *Sanhedrin* (97b) quoted by the Rambam strongly criticizes those who attempt to calculate the date when *Mashiach* will appear. Although the Talmud does mention such calculations, it is obvious that such speculation can only be indulged in by the greatest of our sages. The prophet Habakkuk (2:3) tells us how we should approach *biat hamashiach*:

„אם יתמהמה חכה לו כי יבא ולא יאחר"

"If he tarries wait for him, for he will surely come and he will not be late."

TECHIYAT HAMATIM:
THE RESURRECTION OF THE DEAD

The great climax to *yemot hamashiach* is *techiyat hamatim* when the bodies of the righteous dead will be reunited with their individual souls in an eternal life on this earth. There are many unknowns concerning the mechanics of resurrection, just as there are many secrets concerning creation. But one thing is clear. We have a *masorah* from G-D on Sinai that He will bring back to life the dead. The great stress Chazal placed on this principle is made evident by the Mishna (*Sanhedrin* 90a):

"וֹאֵלוֹ שָׁאֵין לָהֶם חֵלֶק לְעוֹלָם הַבָּא הָאוֹמֵר אֵין תְּחִיַּת הַמֵּתִים מִן הַתּוֹרָה."

"And these do not have a share in the world to come, one who says there is no resurrection of the dead from the Torah."

QUESTION 1 — What is the evidence in Torah *she-bektav* and the Prophets supporting the *masorah* of *techiyat hamatim?*

The Gemara in *Sanhedrin* (90b) quotes several Biblical sources for *techiyat hamatim*. In *Bamidbar* (18:25) Israel is commanded to give *terumah* to Aharon, the Cohen. Since Aharon died before the Jews entered Eretz Yisroel and therefore before the mitzva of *terumah* was in force, the Gemara declares that this *posuk* refers to the end of days, after Aharon's resurrection. Raban Gamliel teaches the following *masorah* for *techiyat hamatim* (*Devarim* 31:16).

„ויאמר ה' אל משה הנך שכב עם אבתיך וקם".

"And G-D said to Moses, behold you will be with your fathers and then rise up." One final source from *Chumash* will suffice, although the Talmud mentions several others. We find the following sentence in *Devarim* (32:39)

„ואני אמית ואחיה מחצתי ואני ארפא".

"I kill and I make alive, I wound and I heal." The Talmud (*Pesachim* 68a) stresses the parallelism of the sentence. Just as G-D heals the very person who has been wounded, so too He makes alive the person who has died. We will quote one of the many sentences in *Tanach* which point to *techiyat hamatim* (Daniel 12:2):

„ורבים מישיני אדמת עפר יקיצו אלה לחיי עולם ואלה לחרפות".

"Many of them that sleep in the dust of the earth shall awake, some to everlasting life, and some to reproaches."

QUESTION 2 — Will the individual be revived as he appeared at death? What about a blind or maimed person? Will *techiyat hamatim* apply only to adults or even to children who died in infancy?

We mentioned above that there are many unknowns concerning the details of *techiyat hamatim*. Man has neither right nor reason to expect G-D to reveal all His secrets. Many answers are beyond human comprehension. Who are we to understand the mysterious way in which G-D works? Nevertheless our great sages do give us some inkling of the world after *techiyat hamatim*. The Gemara in *Pasachim*

(68a) based on the *posuk* quoted above (*Devarim* 32:39) promises that initially man will reappear in the same physical condition as he was prior to death. Thereafter, G-D will heal all physical imperfections. The Ramban expands this concept; once the dead have been revived they will live on in the body for all eternity. But this body after the initial resurrection will not be the present body but a specially refined body, free of all the human weakness which makes the body in *olam hazeh* susceptible to pain, disease and aging.

Similarly, the Gemara in *Sanhedrin* (110b) clearly indicates that *techiyat hamatim* applies to one who died in infancy. The Amoraiim offer several opinions—some holding that even after conception a fetus has a share in the world to come, others require birth, while others require some minimal physical (milah) or intellectual development (the ability to speak). Judaism's view should be contrasted with that of Christianity which condemns an infant who has died before baptism to an eternal Hell. Even the *Amora* who requires some development before the child is eligible for *olam haba* does not suggest that the infant is damned to any eternal Hell.

QUESTION 3 — Our *tefillot* naturally contain many references to the concepts of *olam haba* and *techiyat hamatim*. In *Shachrit* of Shabbat immediately after *Borchu* we recite the beautiful hymn *hakol yoducha* which concludes:

„אין כערכך ה׳ אלקינו בעולם הזה ואין זולתך מלכינו לעולם הבא אפס
בלתך גואלינו לימות המשיח ואין דומה לך מושיענו לתחית המתים״.

Can you translate this selection? Do you recognize the significance of the order of the phrases in this selection?

QUESTION 4 — The first three *brachot* of *Shmoneh Esreh* are known as *birkat shevach*, or "blessings of praise." The second *bracha*, known as *gvurot*, recounts the omnipotence or great power of G-D. What do we single out in this blessing as the most dramatic example of G-D's *gvurah*?

QUESTION 5 — Can you translate these final two sentences from Yigdal?

„ישלח לקץ ימין משיחנו לפדות מחכי קץ ישועתו מתים יחיה אל ברב חסדו ברוך עדי עד שם תהלתו".

LESSON 40

SCHAR V'ONESH: REWARD AND PUNISHMENT

The doctrine of *schar v'onesh*, that man is rewarded for doing good and punished for doing evil, follows inevitably from the principles of *bechirat chafshit* and the justice of G-D. The Rambam includes this doctrine among the thirteen fundamental articles of faith. Throughout the Torah this theme is evident. After Adam and Eve had sinned, their punishment is told them (*Bereshit* 3:16-19); the first murderer, Cain, is told his punishment by G-D (*Bereshit* 4:11-12). Noah and his family alone of all mankind are saved from the flood because they alone merit salvation. Similar illustrations can be found throughout *Tanach.*

QUESTION 1 — What type of reward does the Torah promise for observance of the mitzvot? Why does the Torah mention specified rewards only in several mitzvot?

The Torah promises *arichat yamim,* length of days, and a good life for the observance of honoring one's parents (*Devarim* 5:16), and *shiluach haken,* sending away the mother bird before taking the young (*Devarim* 22:6-7). *Chazal* explain that honoring parents is an obvious expression of gratitude for all that parents do for their children. It is partial payment of a debt which can never be repaid. Similarly, *shiluach haken* is an obvious expression of elementary human kindness which involves neither monetary loss nor any burden. If the Torah promises reward for such *mitzvot kalot*, mitzvot which can easily be performed, how much more *schar* awaits the performance of more demanding and difficult mitzvot.

In the Talmud there appears to be two approaches among *Chazal* concerning the question of *schar*. Rabbi Yaakov (*Kiddushin* 39b) is of the opinion that there is no reward in *olam hazeh* for the observance of the mitzvot. He explains that the above verses refer to *olam haba* and specifically to *techiyat hamatim*. "The world where life is only good, and where life is eternal." But the great majority of *Chazal* are of the opinion that there is reward in *olam hazeh* as well as in *olam haba*. The second parsha of *kriyat shema* which begins "*v'haya im shamoa*"—"And it shall come to pass if you will listen diligently to My commands . . ." And then proceeds to spell out a series of material blessings in this world which follow *shmirat hamitzvot* certainly supports the view that *schar v'onesh* applies to *olam hazeh*. The comment of *Chazal* on the last sentence of this parsha is representative of the majority approach.

‏„'למען ירבו ימיכם' — בעולם הזה, 'וימי בניכם' — בימות המשיח...‏
‏'כימי השמים על הארץ' — בעולם הבא".‏

Certainly the first Mishna in *Peah* which we recite each morning supports this view:

‏„אלו דברים שאדם אוכל פירותיהם בעולם הזה והקרן קימת לו לעולם‏
‏הבא ואלו הן כבוד אב ואם גמילת חסדים והבאת שלום בין אדם לחבירו‏
‏ותלמוד תורה כנגד כולם".‏

QUESTION 2 — Can you translate this Mishna? What does *gemilat chasadim* include? What is the unifying theme of these *mitzvot*? How do these *mitzvot* differ from, for example, tefillin, shabbat, matzo, etc.? Do you have any idea why these mitzvot bring reward both in *olam hazeh* and *olam haba*?

QUESTION 3 — Is there any other way to reconcile the two views of *Chazal*, i.e., Rabbi Yaakov's view and that of the majority concerning reward for the observance of the mitzvot?

The Rambam (*Teshuva* 9:1) explains that the true reward for observing the mitzvot is to be found in *olam haba*. Nevertheless, he argues, the Torah promises that *shmirot hamitzvot* brings with it in *olam hazeh* such things as peace, health, long life and wealth. But these manifestations of the good life in *olam hazeh* are not in their own right the *schar* which is due the righteous. Instead they make possible the performance of further mitzvot so as to enable the individual to accumulate further *schar* which will ultimately be enjoyed in *olam haba*. As an example, when a good man is blessed with wealth in this world that is not the reward due him for his righteousness. This wealth serves as a means to an end; it gives the individual an opportunity to practice the mitzva of *tzadaka* specifically, and all the other *mitzvot*, free from the care and concern of providing for his family's material needs. The same holds true of the other blessings, e.g., health and long life. They make it easier for the *tzadik* to reach that stage of human perfection which entitles him to the ultimate bliss of *olam haba*.

LESSON 41

TZADIK V'RA LO:
THE SUFFERING OF THE RIGHTEOUS

QUESTION 1 — How can we understand the occasional, apparently undeserved suffering of the righteous and happiness of the wicked?

This question, known in the Talmud as the problem of *tzadik v'ra lo, rasha v'tov lo*, has perplexed Jewish thinkers throughout the ages. In fact according to one opinion in the Gemara (*Berakot* 7a), Moshe himself asked G-D for the explanation, only to receive the cryptic reply (*Shmot* 33:13):

„וחנתי את אשר אחן ורחמתי את אשר ארחם"

"I will be gracious to whom I will be gracious and I will show mercy on whom I will show mercy." Similarly, in *Pirke Avot* (4:14) the Tanna Rabbi Yannai comments: "It is not in our power to explain either the prosperity of the wicked or the afflictions of the righteous." It is obvious from these selections that man can not come up with any definite answer to the question. We cannot expect to understand all of G-D's mysterious ways. Furthermore, as the Rambam points out (*Teshuva* 3:2), only G-D can truly evaluate the quality of an individual's deeds or misdeeds. Nevertheless, once we recognize that complete solutions are not possible, it will be beneficial to examine how *Chazal* approach this problem.

QUESTION 2 — If *schar v'onesh* is understood to apply solely to *olam haba* then there is no problem of *tzadik v'ra lo*. The reward due the *tzadik* awaits him in the world to come. But how can the position of the majority of *Chazal* that *schar* is *rewarded* both in *olam hazeh* and *olam haba* be reconciled with *tzadik v'ra lo*?

The first point to be stressed is that outward appearances of success can often be deceiving. Merely because a man has wealth, power, prestige and other trappings of success does not guarantee that he in fact is happy. Conversely, a man poor in money may be rich in far more fundamental and important matters. *Chazal* with their usual incisive insight into human psychology expressed perfectly a fundamental truth of the human condition.

„איזהו עשיר השמח בחלקו"

Nor should we overlook the contribution to personal happiness which commitment to G-D and His Torah brings. Throughout this country, particularly among youth, a deep sense of spiritual malaise and frustration is common. People are searching for some meaning to life, many with no success. How different is the situation of the committed Jew. His life has meaning. His dedication to G-D and the mitzvot enables him to face both life and death with confidence, assured of G-D's mercy and justice.

Some of the great *Rishonim* come to grips with the problems of *tzadik v'ra lo* and *rasha v'tov lo*. Both Rav Saadiah Gaon and the Ramban explain that G-D will occasionally bring suffering to the righteous man in this world as atonement for the few sins he has committed. In this manner he will be able to enter *olam haba* purged of all sin. Saadiah also stresses that there are sufferings of the righteous which are not meant as punishment for past misdeeds. Rather this suffering increases the reward in *olam haba*, especially if the suffering was endured without protest or the hint of rebellion. This is the explanation for the suffering of little children.

Similarly, it is possible that a wicked man who does not deserve *olam haba* has nevertheless done some good deeds for which he deserves reward—reward which can only be given him in *olam hazeh*. Saadiah also lists reasons for the long life which a *rasha* is sometimes granted. At times such long life is meant to give the *rasha* an opportunity to repent; other times it is granted for the sake of righteous people who are closely related to him, or so that he might father a righteous son.

LESSON 42

THE PURPOSE OF THE MITZVOT

QUESTION 1 — What is the purpose of the mitzvot? By this is meant not the purpose of any one specific mitzva, but the whole of halacha. From the eighth day of a boy's life when the mitzva of milah is performed, until the recitation of *Tziduk Hadin* at one's funeral, the observant Jew constantly surrounds himself with the performance of mitzvot. Upon awakening each morning, even before washing our hands, we recite the prayer of *Modeh Ani* and the last thing we do before going to sleep is to recite *keriyat shema al hamita*—throughout the day also we are never far removed from the performance of one of G-D's commands. What role does such an all-encompassing system perform?

Perhaps the best starting point to analyze the function of mitzvot is the famous midrashic statement of Rav (*Bereshit Rabba* 44:1):

„רב אמר לא נתנו המצות אלא לצרף בהן את הבריות"

"Rav said, the mitzvot were given so that mankind would thereby be purified." It is obvious from this selection that mitzvot were given for the benefit of Israel (and thereby all mankind), but what does Rav mean "to purify" mankind?

148

In a previous lesson we saw that the selection of Israel as G-D's chosen people involves two interrelated functions— Israel must first be a *goy kadosh*, "a holy nation" before it can fulfill *mamlechet cohanim*, its priestly mission of spreading G-D's word to the rest of mankind. We also isolated two distinct aspects of *kadosh*. First, *kadosh* means to be separate, distinct from, unique. In order for Israel to be *goy kadosh*, it must be set apart from the other nations with its own unique way of life. This unique way of life in order to proper qualify as *kadosh* must be all pervasive; it must shape and mold all of human activity, both the sacred and the everyday. The second aspect of *kadosh* is perfection—man can reach this state of perfection only if he dedicates his behavior so that it corresponds to the behavior which G-D expects of him. At its most elementary level, then, the mitzvot enable the individual Jew to participate as a member of *am kadosh*, to serve as an example to the rest of mankind.

QUESTION 2 — The term *hekdesh* is used in halachic terminology to describe an article which has been consecrated for the *Bet Hamikdash*. Do you see how the term *hekdesh* includes both aspects of *kadosh*?

There is an important distinction between the attitude of Judaism and that of Christianity concerning the physical side of man's life which leads to a deeper understanding of the role of the mitzvot. According to Christianity there is something inherently sinful about the physical aspects of life. Eating, sex and other such activities are evils, necessary evils to be sure, but evils nonetheless which point up the weakness of man. This explains the stress in Christianity, particularly Catholicism, upon celibacy and various forms of monasticism which practice physical deprivation. Such a view is totally alien to Judaism which bases its attitude upon the following verse (*Bereshit* 2:7):

„וייצר ה' אלקים את האדם עפר מן האדמה ויפח באפיו נשמת חיים..."

"And G-D created man of the dust of the ground and breathed into his nostrils the breath of life." Man is a composite of both *afar haadama* and *nishmat Elokim*—as such he is made up of both the physical and the spiritual. Since each of these two aspects of man was granted by G-D, it is clearly improper to view either as essentially sinful. It is here that the mitzot perform their great role. The purely physical act, performed according to the rules of halacha is infused with *kedusha;* it becomes an expression of man's quest for the divine. The mitzvot provide means to transform simple, physical activities into *avodat Hashem,* the service of the Lord.

QUESTION 3 — Can you explain why in the sentence just quoted, the word *vayizer* appears with two *yudin?*

QUESTION 4 — What is the reason that the Torah requires a *nazir* to bring a *korbon* at the conclusion of his *nazirut?* What type of *korbon* does he bring?

Let us illustrate this process of transforming purely physical activities into *Avodat Hashem* by using "eating" as a model. If the meal is preceeded by the proper *bracha rishona* and followed with the proper *bracha achrona* praising and thanking G-D for his bounty, a mundane everyday activity has become a religious experience. In fact, a meal often becomes in halacha the performance of a mitzva. So, for example, *Chazal* include as part of *oneg* Shabbat and Yom Tov the mitzva of *Shalosh Seudot,* the requirement that we eat three meals on these days. Tosafot quoted *l'halacha* by Rabbi Moshe Isserles in the *Shulchan Aruch (Orach Hayim* 167:15) justifies the custom of bringing salt to the meal-table, and in so doing evokes beautifully the theme with which we have been dealing. He compares our meal-table to the *mizbeach,* the altar in the Temple, since our table is also used for *avodat Hashem*. Just as salt was used on the *mizbeach*, so too it should be found on our tables.

QUESTION 5 — What is meant by *bracha rishona* and bracha *achrona?* Can you identify the various blessings which make up these two categories?

LESSON 43

THE PURPOSE OF THE MITZVOT (Part 2)

The mitzvot as a whole perform another extremely valuable function. In the last lesson we stressed that Judaism, in contrast to other religions, does not view negatively the physical part of man's life. But *yahadut* also recognizes that man's *yetzer*, his physical desires and passions, must be controlled, lest this *yetzer* enslave the individual. The great distinction between human beings and animals is that the latter act instinctively—animals do not have the ability to control their instinctive drive. G-D's great gift to man, the gift of reason, can potentially serve this function. But man's reason does not automatically insure that he will be free of slavery to his *yetzer*. Some mechanism is necessary which will trigger reason so that any particular human act is the product of a reasoned choice rather than a simple response to an instinctive drive. The mitzvot perform this valuable role because they force the individual to stop and consider, to think, before he acts.

QUESTION 1 — There are those who claim that the mitzvot —a series of do's and do not's—cut down on the range of human freedom. Do you realize that this is an extremely narrow and immature approach? Do you understand on the basis of the above analysis how the mitzvot on the contrary perform a liberating function?

Certainly the first and most basic of man's instincts is that of eating. Let us illustrate how the mitzvot make certain that a Jew's choice of food is the product of reason rather than of instinct. Assume that an observant Jew is offered a desirable item of food, does he automatically accept and begin to eat? Definitely not. He must first consider whether or not it is *maachalot assurot,* one of the prohibited foods. Even if it is not of this category, he must then consider whether it may be eaten at that particular time, e.g. it may be a dairy item and he has recently eaten meat, or it may be *chometz* during Pesach. Even if all these obstacles are cleared, the food may not yet be eaten. The individual must stop and acknowledge G-D's bounty by reciting the appropriate blessing.

QUESTION 2 — Various reasons are often advanced to explain a particular food prohibition. So, we are told, pigs are basically unclean and their products often contain bacteria which cause disease. These explanations may or may not be scientifically accurate. Do you realize why such explanations, based on our analysis, are entirely irrelevant? Is the Torah in the halacha pertaining to eating merely attempting to establish hygenic rules? Or does the Torah attempt something far more important, a method to train man to control his most basic instinctive drive?

QUESTION 3 — *Chazal* in Pirke Avot (6:2) express perfectly this theme:

„ואומר 'והלחת מעשה אלקים המה והמכתב מכתב אלקים הוא חרות על הלחות' אל תקרא חרות אלא חרות שאין לך בן חורין אלא מי שעוסק בתלמוד תורה"

What do Chazal mean when they suggest that this verse be understood as if it read *cherut?*

LESSON 44

REFLECTIONS ON THE MITZVOT

We know that the Torah contains *taryag* or 613 mitzvot, 365 mitzvot *lo taaseh*, or negative prohibitions, and 248 *aseh*, or positive commandments. The Talmud (*Makkot* 23b) tells us that the former correspond to the number of days in the year and the latter correspond to the different parts of the human body. We have already seen in lesson 12 that the *Rabbanan* with the full approval of the Torah enacted many other laws.

QUESTION 1 — What is the reason for this great multitude of mitzvot? Furthermore, many of the Torah's laws, such as the requirement to honor and respect one's parents or the prohibition against murder and theft, are so obvious and reasonable that even without G-D's command man would instinctively arrive at the proper course of behavior. If so why was it necessary for the Torah to stamp such laws with the force of G-D's command?

The Mishna (*Makkot* 23b) answers this question:

‏"רב חנניא בן עקשיא אומר רצה הקב"ה לזכות את ישראל לפיכך הרבה
להם תורה ומצוות..."

Rashi explains that some of the mitzvot would have been observed even if the Torah had not mentioned them. The purpose of mentioning these acts in the Torah was to transform them from acts sanctioned merely by human reason to acts commanded by G-D. Because of this transformation a Jew who refrains from a *lo taaseh* and performs an *aseh* merits the reward which is due one who observed a mitzva. That is why the Mishna refers to this process as a *zchut;* it is an example of G-D's benevolence to His people. The Jew is granted *schar* for behavior which even if not commanded, would have been followed.

The mitzvot of the Torah may be divided into two categories, *mishpatim* and *chukkim. Mishpatim* are those mitzvot whose purpose is immediately apparent to human reason. Included in this category are the prohibitions against murder, theft, idolatry, incest, adultery and the requirements to give charity and practice righteousness, to respect one's parents, to pray and all the mitzvot which lead to *kedusha. Chukkim,* on the other hand, serve no apparent purpose. Included in this category are such mitzvot as *orla* which prohibits enjoyment of the fruit of trees for the first three years after planting, *shatnes* which prohibits the mixture of wool and linen, the prohibition of cooking meat and milk together, and of course *para aduma,* the red heifer found in the Temple service.

QUESTION 2 — Do we believe that each *chok* has a practical purpose although that purpose is not readily ascertainable? In the alternative, is the sole purpose of *chukkim* to serve as a clear indication of the Jew's obedience and submission to the command of his Creator?

Certainly *chukkim* are as important and binding upon the Jew as logical, rational laws. We observe the mitzvot, all mitzvot, because it is G-D's will. We have neither right nor reason to question G-D's command. It is pure arrogance for man to expect G-D to reveal the reason behind His mitzvot.

Nevertheless Jewish philosophers agree that there is a reason and purpose underlying each of the *taryag* mitzvot. The Rambam's opinion is clear from the following selection in the "*Moreh Nevuchim*" (3:31): "Every one of the six hundred and thirteen precepts serves to inculcate some truth, to remove some erroneous opinion, to establish proper relations in society, to diminish evil, to train in good manners, or to warn against bad habits."

QUESTION 3 — Should man attempt through his rational power to discover the true meaning of the *chukkim?* Put another way, is there a religious duty to attempt to understand and explain all the mitzvot?

This question has produced somewhat different approaches among Jewish philosophers. According to the Rambam in *Yad Hachazaka* (*Meilah*, 7:5) there is such a positive duty. "It is proper for man to reflect upon the laws of the Torah and understand their purpose to the utmost of his ability." Rav Yehuda Halevi in the "Kuzari," however, does not suggest such a duty on the individual's part. Although he does not deny that reason and purpose are at the root of every mitzva, man's basic job is to observe G-D's commands and not to speculate on the reasons.

QUESTION 4 — Why were the reason underlying individual mitzvot often not revealed in the Torah? What possible purpose can this serve?

LESSON 45

SYMBOLIC MITZVOT

All cultures employ symbols to represent ideas. These symbols take many forms—a sign, a word, an act, a particular type of dress. So, for example, a combination of letters represent a word; a dove has traditionally symbolized peace; men shake hands upon departing as a symbol of friendship and unity despite physical separation; soldiers wear ribbons as a sign of past bravery or ordeal. In each of these common instances, an abstract concept is concretized by the use of a symbol, inherently meaningless, but full of meaning once people make the association between the symbol and the concept it represents.

Judaism also uses symbols in the form of symbolic mitzvot to impress upon the Jew many of its fundamental truths. But there is a great difference between the ordinary symbols common to all mankind and the mitzvot. The man-made symbols are inherently meaningless; their sole function is to represent and bring to mind a particular concept. The mitzvot, in contrast, are G-D's creation. Hence besides their symbolic meaning, they inherently possess some utilitarian value.

QUESTION 1 — In previous lessons in this book we analyzed the halacha of shabbat. What symbolic role does refraining from melacha serve? The mitzva of *shmita* requires the Jew to leave his soil in Eretz Yisroel fallow every seventh year. What is the symbolic meaning of this mitzva? Every male Jew whose physical condition permits is circumcised on the eighth day of his life. What is the symbolic significance of the *brit milah*?

QUESTION 2 — Each of the three mitzvot mentioned in question 1 has an important utilitarian purpose besides its symbolic meaning. What is the practical value of each of of these mitzvot? Were the respective utilitarian purposes of these mitzvot always recognized by mankind? What does this suggest concerning other symbolic mitzvot?

In the remainder of this lesson and in the lessons which follow we shall analyze the symbolic content of various mitzvot. Let us begin with two mitzvot which deal with eating —chometz on Pesach and *gid hanasheh*. You should of course recall the role common to all such mitzvot, viz., imposing self-discipline over man's most basic physical drive.

The Torah in *Bereshit* (32:24) recounts Jacob's struggle in the dead of night with a mysterious stranger, identified by Chazal as Esau's guardian angel. As dawn approaches Jacob although wounded in the thigh, prevails and his blessing is confirmed. To commemorate this event the Torah prohibits our eating the *gid hanasheh*, the sciatic nerve of an animal's hindquarter. This struggle between Jacob and Esau's angel is a model of the constant struggle throughout history between Israel and its enemies. The limping Jacob who emerges from the encounter as victorious Israel is a symbol of *Am Yisroel*. We will never be ultimately defeated by the superior force of Esau, although like Yaakov we may suffer from wounds and temporary pain and suffering in our battle with our enemies.

QUESTION 3 — What fundamental truth do we symbolically affirm by refraining from eating *gid hanasheh?*

The Jew's abstinence from *chometz* on Pesach similarly has profound symbolic significance. The Torah tells us that the *chometz* prohibition is due to the fact that *Bnei Yisroel* had no time to wait for the fermentation of dough when they departed from Egypt. Logically, this fact is not sufficiently important in itself to warrant its eternal commemoration. However, after a little reflection its significance becomes evident. A mass of two million people leave Egypt to journey in the desolate wilderness for an unknown duration without any preparation of food. Would any human leader dare lead such a mission with starvation a certain result? Would the people themselves follow a human leader in view of such certain consequences? Rather the Torah wishes to emphasize the absolute faith and trust which Israel placed in G-D when they left Egypt in such haste that they had no time to bake bread. It is this point which the Torah stresses in the following posuk (*Shmot* 12:17):

„ושמרתם את המצות כי בעצם היום הזה הוצאתי את צבאותיכם מארץ
מצרים ושמרתם את היום הזה לדרתיכם חקת עולם."

"You shall watch the matzot for on this very day I brought your hosts out of the land of Egypt; therefore you shall keep this day throughout your generations a statute forever." When Jews observe the laws of *chometz* to this day they symbolically express, as their ancestors before them did, their faith in divine guidance in Israel's history.

LESSON 46

TEFILLIN, MEZUZA AND TZITZIT

In a previous lesson (29) the mitzva of tefillin was used to illustrate the methodology of Torah *she-beal peh* in arriving at the true halacha. In this lesson we deal with the symbolic purpose of this and related mitzvot. The Torah tells us that Tefillin are a sign and remembrance of the covenant relationship between G-D and the *am hanivchar*.

(שמות י"ג:ט') „והיה לך לאות על ידך ולזכרון בין עיניך..."

Both the Tefillin *shel yad* and the *shel rosh* consist of four *parshiyot* or sections from the Torah. These four *parshiyot* are:

(a) *Kadesh* (*Shmot* 13:1-10) which recounts G-D's role in Israel's redemption from Egyptian slavery.
(b) *V'haya ki yeviacha* (*Shmot* 13:11-16) which requires each Jew to teach his children the Torah.
(c) *Shema* (*Devarim* 6:4-9) which contains the affirmation of G-D's unity and the acceptance of His mitzvot.
(d) *V'haya im shamoa* (*Devarim* 11:13-21) which contains G-D's assurance of the reward which follows our observance of the mitzvot and warns of the punishment which disobedience brings.

160

QUESTION 1 — The Torah requires that the tefillin be worn on the left bicep (for a right-handed person) midway between the elbow and shoulder, and on the head where the hairline begins. What is the symbolic significance of these particular places?

Wearing tefillin on the head, the place of man's brain, suggests that we dedicate our intellect and rational faculty to G-D's will. Similarly, the location of the left bicep is particularly appropriate. Both the arm, which represents man's actions, and the heart, which represents our emotions and desires, are symbolically placed into G-D's service.

QUESTION 2 — Why do we not put on tefillin on *Shabbat* and *Yom Tov?* Why do some Jews wear tefillin on *Chol Hamoed*, while others do not?

QUESTION 3 — In both the *parshot* of *shema* and *v'haya im shamoa* immediately after the verse which deals with tefillin, we find the mitzva of placing a mezuza on one's doorposts. The halacha requires that a mezuza be placed in the entrance of each room in one's home (except for the bathroom). What is the significance of requiring a mezuza in each room?

Closely related to these mitzvot is the mitzva of *tzitzit*. The Torah very clearly indicates the symbolic function of *tzitzit* (*Bamidbar* 15:39-40):

„והיה לכם לציצית וראיתם אותו וזכרתם את כל מצות ה' ועשיתם אותם ולא תתורו אחרי לבבכם ואחרי עיניכם אשר אתם זנים אחריהם... והייתם קדשים לאלקיכם."

Tzitzit are a constant reminder of the Jew's requirement to act as a member of *am kodesh*. The Talmud (*Menachot* 43b) explains that seeing and apprehending the *tzitzit* leads to *zechira* and *asiya* of the other mitzvot.

QUESTION 4 — What is the numerical value of the letters which comprise the word *tzitzit?* What is the significance of this question?

The close interrelationships between the three mitzvot discussed in this lesson are made apparent by the following Talmudic statement in *Menachot* (23b):

„כל שיש לו תפילין בראשו ותפילין בזרועו וציצית בבגדו ומזוזה בפתחו
הכל בחיזוק שלא יחטא.״

"An individual who has tefillin on his head and tefillin on his arm, *tzitzit* on his garment, and mezuzah on his doorway, he is certain not to sin." For these mitzvot constantly surround the Jew; they shield him from any temptation; they are a constant reminder of his obligation to his Creator.

QUESTION 5 — Can you think of at least one other practice which provides the same function of constantly reminding the Jew of who he is and how he must act?

LESSON 47

SHATNES

It is a curious phenomenon of contemporary Jewish life in America that many Jews who are careful to observe properly the mitzvot are at the same time lax concerning one specific mitzva *deoraitha*. I am referring to the law of shatnes which prohibits the mixture of wool and linen in any garment. There is no logical explanation for this sad occurrence, but it nevertheless remains a fact. In this lesson we will attempt to pinpoint the important symbolism of this mitzva in an attempt to correct this deplorable situation.

QUESTION 1 — If a garment is labeled "100% pure wool" is there any need to have it checked for shatnes? Ask your teacher for the procedure to be followed in your locality.

QUESTION 2 — Does the law of shatnes apply only to garments worn by men, or does it apply equally to women's clothing?

Ordinarily shatnes is classified as a *chok* based upon the *posuk* (*Vayikra* 19:19) from which it is derived:

„את חקתי תשמרו בהמתך לא תרביע כלאים שדך לא תזרע כלאים ובגד
כלאים שעטנז לא יעלה עליך"

"You shall keep my ordinances, you shall not mate two

kinds of your animals, you shall not sow your field with two
kinds of seeds, nor shall a garment woven of linen and wool
come upon you."

The Talmud (*Sanhedrin* 60a) offers an important insight
into this mitzva.

„אמר קרא 'את חקתי תשמרו' חוקים שחקקתי לך כבר."

Many commentators explain that these *chukim* refer to the
laws of nature established by G-D during the six days of
creation. In the first chapter of *Bereshit* the Torah states
that each different type in the vegetable and animal kingdoms is to bear fruit and reproduce *l'mineihu*, in accordance
with its own species. The Ramban (*Vayikra* 19:19) explains
that the three categories of *kilayim* or prohibited mixtures
found in this *posuk* impress upon man that he cannot improve upon G-D's creation. The three prohibitions cover the
full range of potential activity. The first, *kilayei beheima*,
prohibits the interbreeding of different animals. The next,
kelayei zeraim, prohibits the intermingling of seeds. Shatnes
completes this scheme by prohibiting the mixture of wool,
which comes from sheep, and linen, which is derived from
flax. In other words the law of shatnes prohibits the joining
of products of the animal and vegetable worlds.

The three *kilayim mitzvot* perform an important educa-
tive function. They are a symbolic reminder of man's technological limits. G-D, the creator, established rules of nature;
we are not to tamper with them.

QUESTION 3 — Will attempts at breeding a cat with a dog
be successful? Can related species, e.g., a horse and donkey,
produce offspring? What is the character of such offspring?
What does this suggest concerning the nature of creation?

QUESTION 4 — What is the derivation of the Hebrew word
shatnes?

LESSON 48

THE STATUS OF WOMEN IN JUDAISM

The status of women in the halachic system has produced a great deal of misunderstanding and misconception. Occasionally the view is expressed that Judaism relegates women to a position of inferiority. This view results from an erroneous understanding of two subjects: a) the religious duties of men are more extensive than those of women; b) the requirement of a mechitza or partition which separates the men's and women's section in the synagogue. Accordingly, in this lesson these two subjects will be analyzed in order to place the entire topic in its proper perspective.

We have seen that the Torah's mitzvot are divided into 365 mitzvot *lo taaseh*, negative commandments, and 248 *aseh*, positive commandments. Each of the mitzvot *lo taaseh* applies with equal force to women (with the obvious exception of the shaving prohibitions which are not applicable). It is only within the category of mitzvot *aseh*—and furthermore only within a specific subdivision of such mitzvot—that we find distinctions between the obligations of men and women. Those mitzvot *aseh* which do not depend upon time, e.g., *mezuza, tzedaka* and many others which are based on humane and righteous behavior also apply equally to women. Only mitzvot *aseh she-hazman gerama*, i.e., those mitzvot which

165

must be performed at a particular time, either a specific time of day or a particular day of the year, are not obligatory.

Question 1 — Is there any reason why these mitzvot are not binding on women?

Rishonim explain that an extremely practical reason underlines the exemption of women from these mitzvot which are bound to specific times. Simply put a woman's time is not her own. Her first responsibility is to her family, caring for and tending to her children. The woman's exemption from these mitzvot, then, is not the result of any lack of equality. Rather, it reflects woman's natural superiority in raising and training children—a task so important that it even transcends certain mitzvot.

Question 2 — Can women fulfill these mitzvot and receive *schar* for their observance? If so may they recite the ordinary blessing *asher kidishanu be'mitzvotav v'tzevanu* . . . ? What Mitzvot *aseh she-hazman gerama* are commonly observed by Jewish women?

Question 3 — Which mitzvot *aseh she-hazman gerama* are binding on women? What are the reasons for these exceptions to the general rule?

Question 4 — Is the practice of separating the sexes in the synagogue with a *mechitza* a *minhag*, a custom, or a *din*, an obligatory law? Is it a relatively recent innovation or an ancient practice?

The traditional separate seating arrangement in the synagogue has been followed by Jews throughout history, and throughout the world. It is only within the past century that any breach appeared in the uniform, accepted practice. It can be traced back to the *Bet Hamikdash*. The Talmud

(*Succah* 51b) in reference to the *simchat bet hashoeva* celebration in the Temple during Sukkot explains that a balcony was built to seat the women who came to the Temple to watch the celebration, and to prevent any mingling of the sexes. Such an addition to the *Bet Hamikdash* would be proper only if the separation of the sexes is a Biblical requirement, a *din deoraitha*. The Talmud in several places (e.g., *Megilla* 29a) indicates that our synagogues are to be compared to a *mikdash meat*, a Temple in miniature. Thus, according to one opinion in the Gemara the daily prayers were instituted in place of the daily sacrifices. If our synagogues are to retain their character of *mikdash meat*, they must conform to the traditional practice.

QUESTION 5 — Why does the halacha require the separation of the sexes? What positive role do the separate sections divided by a *mechitza* serve?

The synagogue service serves one function and one function only. It is a place of prayer, a place for a religious experience and not a social experience. The halacha is designed to produce true *kavanah* which we have already defined as the *mithpallel's* realization that he stands in the presence of G-D. In order to achieve *kavanah* all possible sources of distraction must be eliminated. During prayer man must be alone with G-D. The words of a contemporary *gadol* are particularly apt. "Clearly, the presence of women among men, or of men among women, which often evokes a certain frivolity in the group, either in spirit or in behavior, can contribute little to sanctification or to the deepening of religious feeling; nor can it help to instill that mood in which a man must be immersed when he would communicate with the Almighty."

TEACHER'S GUIDE

LESSONS 1 & 2

CREATION: ACCIDENT OR PURPOSEFUL

The first two lessons of this volume draw upon the argument of design advanced by virtually all philosophers of religion, both Jewish and non-Jewish, to make out a forceful case for the truth of G-D's existence. Essentially there are but two answers proposed to explain the existence of the world. Religion attributes all to the planned, purposeful direction of an omnipotent G-D. Materialistic atheism attributes all to the directionless, random working of pure chance. With some reflection and proper guidance it should not be too difficult to expose to the student the flaws inherent in the pure chance theory. Even Darwin, certainly no ally of religion, was so impressed by the argument of design that he was led to write: "I am conscious that I am in an utterly hapless muddle (concerning the argument of design) . . . Again I say, I am and shall ever remain in a hapless muddle." ("Life and Letters," Vol. II, p. 353.)

How can we go about exposing these flaws in the materialistic theory? First, we must indicate how enormously numbers multiply when dealing with chance. Question 1 of the first lesson which deals with selecting pennies from a box is designed to do just that. The chance of drawing number 1 is 1 in 10. The chance of drawing 1 and 2 in succession would be 1 in 100 (1 in 10 times 1 in 10). The chance of drawing 1, 2, and 3 in succession progresses geometrically to 1 in 1,000 and so on, until the chances of selecting 1 through 10 in succession reaches the unbelievable figure of 1 chance in 10 billion. In the first lesson a cursory attempt is made to indicate the perfect exactness of earth. The teacher should constantly stress that a relatively minor variation in any of the given examples would make life impossible. Students should be asked to augment the examples provided with those of their own. Eventually the student should conclude that the possibility of the world existing purely by accident is no more reasonable than the example provided in question 3, i.e., ink accidentally falling in such a manner as to produce a book. This popular analogy has often been used by Jewish philosophers to prove the existence of G-D. The words of Bahya ibn Pakuda, in *"Chovot Halevavot"* (1:6) are representative: "Do you not realise that if ink were poured out accidentally on a sheet of paper, it would be impossible that proper writing should result, or legible lines such as written with a pen? If a person brought us a fair copy of a script that could only have been written with a pen, and said that the ink had been spilt on paper and these written characters had come of themselves, we would charge him to his face with falsehood, for we would feel certain that this result could not have happened without an intelligent person's purpose. Since this appears to us an impossibility in the case of characters the form of which is conventional, how can one assert that something, far finer in its art, and which manifests in its fashioning a subtlety infinite, beyond comprehension, could have happened without the purpose, power, and wisdom of a wise and mighty designer?"

Question 2 is designed to point out that the scientist necessarily reaches a point where he has no answers. As Dr. Aron Barth has indicated in his classic, "The Modern Jews

Faces Eternal Problems" (p. 27): "In every serious book on such research (research into the manner in which the universe came into existence) it is said explicitly or implicitly 'We can bring you up to a certain point, with a greater or smaller measure of certainty, but beyond that point we cannot go.'" Science faces the very same problem (as will be discussed in future lesson) when dealing with the theory of evolution. Given the existence of lower forms of life, they posit the theory of evolution development. But they admit an inability to explain the existence of these lower forms of life.

The second lesson reiterates the theme of the prior one, but from a different point of view. Whereas lesson 1 focused attention on the mathematical impossibility of the materialistic approach, lesson 2 positively stresses the only other alternative. The text of the Student's Guide accompanying question 2 quotes in translation the famous midrashic teaching of Rabbi Akiva. Throughout this volume such selections often appear in translation in the Student's Guide with the original quotation in the Teacher's Guide. It is my firm belief that such *maamorei* Chazal which contain the fundamentals of Jewish *hashkafa* should, if time permits, be taught to the student in the original Hebrew.

„מעשה שבא מין ואמר לר׳ עקיבא העולם הזה מי בראו? אמר ליה הקב״ה. אמר ליה הראיני דבר ברור... אמר ליה מה אתה לובש? א״ל בגד. א״ל מי עשאו? א״ל האורג. א״ל איני מאמינך הראיני דבר ברור. א״ל ומה אראה לך ואין אתה יודע שהאורג עשאו? א״ל ואתה אינך יודע שהקב״ה ברא את עולמו? נפטר אותו המין. אמרו לו תלמידיו מה הדבר ברור, אמר להם בני כשם שהבית מודיע על הבנאי והבגד מודיע על האורג והדלת על הנגר כך העולם מודיע על הקב״ה שהוא בראו".

Up to this point no distinction has been made between the religious belief and the theism arrived at by certain philosophers. Question 3 corrects that omission. The student's attention is directed to the first blessing of the evening services which details G-d's role in directing down to the minutest detail the complex functioning of the universe. It would be most beneficial if the teacher reviews with the class the full text of the blessing. It is particularly striking that the text appears in the present tense. Judaism does not view G-d as a "prime mover" who, at one point in time, established the natural order and then withdrew from the world. Rather G-d is an active, present participant in the world's affairs. This point must be stressed to the student since it goes to the very foundation of much of our belief. We shall of course return to this theme in later sections of this work.

LESSON 3

AGE OF THE EARTH

It has been my experience that one of the most trouble-some sore points for the Yeshiva student is the apparent conflict between our calendar and the scientific claim that the earth is several billions of years old. What appears to most of us as at worst a trifling problem, becomes for the student a philosophic question of major import. How are we to resolve this apparent contradiction?

In this lesson several alternate solutions are explored. First, doubt is cast on the scientific claim that the earth in fact is several billion years old. It should be stressed to the student that this claim is theory, not fact, and as such is subject to criticism. As indicated in the Student's Guide, the very basis for the theory depends upon an assumption which by its very nature is unverifiable, i.e., that the rate of disintegration has remained constant from the beginning of time until the present. Question 2 is the result of a conversation I had sometime ago with an eminent Jewish scientist. It was his contention that serious doubt may be cast on the validity of the scientific theory. It is known that extreme heat and pressure magnify enormously the rate of chemical reactions. Who can testify to the enormous heat and pressure which might very well have been generated during the creation? Similarly, Chazal indicate that the water of the flood was both scalding and of high sulphuric content. (Cf. *Sanhedrin* 108a and Rashi, *Bereshit* 6:14.) It is of course impossible to calculate the effects of such an environment over an extended period of time on the earth's crust.

Question 3 attempts to reconcile the traditional Jewish calendar with the scientific theory. The Midrash indicates that the Jewish counting of time does not begin from the first second of creation. In fact, according to the Midrash, G-d created and then destroyed previous worlds until He was satisfied with the creation of the world as we know it. This Midrashic statement of course has important ramifications not only concerning the question of time, but also concerning the existence of fossils of animals unknown to us. It is entirely possible that these fossils are the remains of these earlier creations.

(בראשית רבה פרשה ג':ז') "אריי' בר סימון יהי ערב אין כתיב כאן אלא 'ויהי ערב' מכאן שהיה סדר זמנים קודם לכן, א"ר אבהו מלמד שהיה בורא עולמות ומחריבן עד שברא את אלו אמר דין הניין לי יתהון לא הניין לי".

Question 4 introduces a third reconciliation between the traditional Jewish calendar and the scientific evidence which suggests an enormously older earth. The scientific theory assumes that the earth began in a virgin state. But once *maaseh bereshit* is accepted, there is every reason to assume that the earth was created in a mature state. Just as Adam does not first appear as a newly born infant, so, too, the earth would not first have appeared in a new-born state. It therefore follows that the lead we find today in rocks is not necessarily the result of the decomposition of original uranium.

LESSONS 4, 5

EVOLUTION OR CREATION

The topic analyzed in the preceding lesson, although important, is not crucial to the student's *hashkafa*. However, the question of evolution or creation goes to the very core of religion. It must therefore be handled carefully and in great detail. The evidence amassed by responsible scientists to support the theory of evolution is substantial in its own right. But it becomes far more impressive when supplemented by a host of half-truths, the product of popular pseudo-science. What is particularly dangerous from our point of view is that the grade school student does not come into contact with a balanced, critical presentation of the scientific evidence. Instead he reads his school textbooks and sees the mass media which accept evolution as *l'havdil Torah min shamayim*.

Lesson 4 directs the student's attention to two serious problems found in evolutionary theory. It is safe to assume that our students have never had such criticisms pointed out to them. Science has not been able to solve the critical question of the origin of life. Evolution assumes the existence of simple forms of life and then proceeds to develop a theory based on this assumption. Question 1 is designed to point out to the student that the alternative to creation adduced by science, i.e., spontaneous generation, requires just as much an act of faith as does the religious solution. (The Talmud *Shabbat* 107b appears to accept spontaneous generation. Several extremely satisfactory explanations have been offered which reconcile the Talmudic statement with the findings of modern science.) In fact, T. H. Huxley, certainly no friend of religion, and indeed one of its staunchest foes, is forced to reach this conclusion: "I find no record of the commencement of life, and therefore I am devoid of any means of forming a definite conclusion as to the conditions of its appearance. Belief, in the scientific sense of the word, is a serious matter and needs strong foundation. To say, therefore, in the admitted absence of evidence, that I have any belief as to the mode in which existing forms of life have originated would be using words in a wrong sense . . . I should expect to be a witness of the evolution of living protoplasm from not living matter . . . That is the expectation to which reasoning leads me; but I beg you once more to recollect that I have no right to call my opinion anything but an act of philosophical faith."

Question 2 raises the problem of whether the small, individual variations, which Darwin explained result purely by chance, are inheritable. Recent scientific experimentation has shown that the effects of use and disuse of organs which produce modification are not necessarily inheritable. The reproductive cell of an organism is derived solely from the reproductive cell of its parent. Its characteristics do not depend upon the rest of the parent's body, and nothing that happened to the parent's body is transmitted to the offspring. Laboratory experimentation has shown that cutting the tails off generation after generation of mice has no effect whatever on the tail lengths of subsequent generations. Jews have practiced circumcision for thousands of years and yet the practice has produced no change in Jewish babies.

The remainder of lesson 4 is concerned with the strongest rational argument for a belief in a divine creator, and therefore the best refutation of the theory that human life developed purely by chance from single cell organisms. The human mind recoils at the idea that the perfectly exact, complex and intricate coordination found in the human being resulted purely by chance. Digestion has been selected as an illustration of the complexity of human processes. The student should be asked to develop other illustrations, e.g., sight and hearing, etc.

The final question involves the text of *asher yatzar*. This blessing of thanksgiving to G-d for having created man in His infinite wisdom details to some extent both the complexity and frailty of the human body.

Lesson 5 examines several specific aspects of evolutionary theory. According to Darwin, evolution proceeds by small, almost imperceptible modifications. This should produce no great gaps in the evolutionary scale. Yet no one can deny the great difference which exists between man and the highest forms of animal life. Furthermore, the missing link which would bridge the gap between ape and man has never been found. It has become such an article of faith among some scientists that in their zeal they have succumbed more than once and loudly proclaimed finds, only to be sorely disappointed when these finds were exposed as cruel hoaxes.

In fact if remains of ape-like men were to be found, I do not think that it would produce any problem to Jewish thought. The Midrash, written more than a thousand years prior to the first fossil finds, teaches that in the age of Enosh, as punishment for having perverted their G-dly image (*tzelem Elokim*), G-d changed them into ape-like creatures.

(בראשית רבה כ"ג:ו') 'ולשת גם הוא יולד בן ויקרא את שמו אנוש...
אמר [אבא כהן ברדלא] עד כאן בצלם ובדמות [אלקים] מכאן ואילך
נתקלקלו הדורות ונבראו קינטורין [מהופכים כקופות], ד' דברים נשתנו
בימי אנוש בן שת... ונעשו פניהם כקופות."

This continued until the days of Noach.

Certainly the most famous argument for the evolutionary theory is based on the existence of fossils. In lesson 5
two explanations are offered. Question 3 suggests that the
fossils may be the remains of life destroyed in the great
flood. Commentaries of the Chumash have explained that
after the flood G-d decreed that sexual union between members of different species could no longer produce offspring
which would be abominable to the creation, although such
hybrid creatures were possible before. This of course would
explain the existence of fossils of animals unknown to us.
Question 1 offers a different solution, i.e., the world at the
moment of creation contained such fossils. I have already
suggested in the Teacher's Guide to lesson 3 that the existence of fossils may be explained as the remains of the
earlier worlds destroyed by G-d mentioned in the Midrash.
This raises the question of why G-d would wish to place
such fossils in our world, i.e., question 2. Although such
speculation is ordinarily futile, and perhaps improper, I
think an attempt should be made in this case. It is necessary
to introduce a theme to be developed fully in the next lesson. G-d does not clearly reveal His presence to man. The
world is so constructed that it contains tests of man's faith,
so that our faith may prevail over our intellectual doubts,
and we may thereby be worthy of G-d's reward. It is certainly
possible that fossils were purposefully placed on this earth
as a test of man's faith in G-d the creator.

The final question focuses attention on the philosophical
and ethical implications of the evolutionary theory. Darwin's
"survival of the fittest" has no ethical connotation; fittest

does not mean best. Hard-shelled crabs, for example, might conceivably survive, and men perish, should the earth cool to a certain point. The theory leaves no room for any idealistic notion of the dignity of man. Darwinism leads naturally to political theories stressing race (Hegel) and the superman (Nietzsche) which in the twentieth century led ultimately to Nazi ideology.

LESSONS 6, 7

MIRACLES

In these two lessons dealing with miracles, our primary task is to make the student aware of *Yad Hashem*, the hand of G-d, as a controlling force in historic events. The Yeshiva student is often troubled by the contrast which he perceives between the many miracles mentioned in Tanaach and the apparent lack of an observable "G-d's hand" in contemporary life. Our task has been made far easier since this generation has been blessed to witness the Jewish history of the past two decades.

The first question in lesson 6 refers to the comment of Rashi on *Bereshit* (6:15) which explains the extended period provided for the construction of the ark as giving the people an opportunity to repent and correct their ways.

The approach of the Ramban, i.e., that miracles conform as much as possible to the natural order is fundamental to Jewish theological thought. Lesson 6, question 2, raises the question of the rationale behind this phenomenon. Why does G-d not reveal His presence to mankind with continued, open and clear miracles? The discussion at the outset of lesson 7 is meant as the response to this perplexing question. If the Jew is to merit reward, he must be confronted with a free choice between selecting the way of Torah and some other way of life. If G-d's presence was continually made manifest—so that no rational man could deny His existence—then man would be no better than a robot, and deservant of no more reward than a machine. Lesson 7, question 1, points out that it is the element of *b'chira chofshit*, free-will, which distinguishes man from the angels.

The answer to the final question of lesson 6 is self-evident. Since supernatural events are disguised in a natural order, it becomes extremely difficult to recognize individual, unusual events as miracles. It was indicated in the student's guide that the perspective provided by reflection over an extended period of time is necessary before G-d's role becomes evident. Questions 2 and 3 are designed to get the student to apply this theme to contemporary events. One unsympathetic to religion will not be convinced that Jewish history of the past several decades evidences clearly G-d's direction of the course of history. The concept of *Yad Hashem* is too sublime to be reduced to mathematical certainty. But the vast majority of our students are not unsympathetic; they are more than eager to be shown. I would suggest that the teacher discuss each facet of recent Jewish history, e.g. the holocaust, the War of Liberation, the Sinai Campaign, the Six-Day War, etc., both as an isolated historical incident and then as individual pieces forming a complex pattern. Taken individually, each of these events may be understood as within the natural course of history, but taken in their totality, they form a pattern which defies a natural explanation and compels the conclusion of G-d's intervention.

The lesson concludes with an illustration provided by Dr. Aron Barth ("The Modern Jew Faces Eternal Problems," pp. 114-15) that miracles can be found in mundane, every-day occurrences. This leads directly to a consideration of the text of *Modim* (question 4). The commentaries of the Siddur explain that *nisecha* refers to personal miracles of which the individual is cognizant, while *nifleotecha* refers to the multitude of favors bestowed by G-d upon an unaware recipient. Certainly it is not an empty phrase when we give thanks "for the miracles that are daily with us."

LESSON 8

SHABBAT: MORE THAN A DAY OF REST

In the several lessons dealing with Sabbath, I have attempted to accomplish two things. First, the basic concepts which comprise Shabbat's philosophic rationale have been analyzed. Then, I have attempted to relate the halacha of Shabbat to these underlying themes. Much of the material developed in these lessons was influenced by "The Sabbath," a small, but extremely valuable volume, written by Dayan Dr. I. Grunfeld.

At the outset of the discussion, I have tried to indicate the fundamental role played by Shabbat as the cornerstone of our faith. It is the key "sign" established by G-d as testimony to the unique relationship between Him and *K'lal Israel*. An analogy of the Chofetz Chaim captures perfectly the role of the "sign." Every storekeeper places a sign at his store to indicate to the public both the nature of the business and that it is a going concern. Even if the owner should leave for some time and close shop, the sign remains to indicate that he remains in business and intends to reopen. But if the owner removes his sign, he shows thereby that he has closed the store permanently. Shabbat is such a sign. Even if a Jew violates some commandments he has not thereby lost his Jewishness. The temporary absence of the storekeeper does not mean that the store is permanently closed. As long as he keeps the sign, the Shabbat, he remains in business. But once he desecrates the Sabbath, he removes the sign, he abandons his religion.

Question 1 introduces two separate motifs found in Judaism. There can be no doubt that Judaism combines both universal and nationalistic tendencies. G-d is the creator of all mankind; He entered into a covenant with Noah and all his sons, that is, with all mankind. He established the seven Noachite laws which apply to all people. At the same time G-d established a unique relationship with the Children of Israel. In theory that aspect of Shabbat which testifies to the creation applies equally to all people. Yet until the personal command to Israel to keep the Sabbath, mankind, with the exception of Abraham and his descendants, did not develop any concept of a Sabbath. It is Israel's task through their observance of Shabbat to make known to all mankind the unity of G-d.

The Tefillot of Shabbat reflect this dualism. In *Tefillat Arvit*, which stresses the universality of Shabbat, the basic theme is Shabbat as a *zecher lemaase bereshit*. The Biblical quotation recited is

„ויכולו השמים והארץ..."

In *Tefillat Shachrit* the focus shifts to the nationalistic motif represented by the statement

„ישמח משה במתנת חלקו..."

The Biblical quotation recited is

„ושמרו בני ישראל את השבת..."

At this point the teacher might find it advisable to discuss with his class the seven Noachite laws. The observance of these mitzvot is the minimum required for acceptable human behavior. The Talmud (Sanhedrin 56b, 57a) lists them: *avodah zarah*—idolatry, *birkat Hashem*—blasphemy, *shfichat damim*—murder, *giluy arayot*—adultery and incest, *gezel*—robbery, *dinim*—establishment of courts which enforce the other six commandments, *ever min hachay*—eating flesh cut from a living animal. However, this discussion may be postponed to a later lesson which will be devoted in its entirety to an analysis of the universalism and nationalism within Judaism.

LESSONS 9, 10

THE HALACHA OF SHABBAT

In this lesson the theme of Shabbat has been developed. By refraining from creative work the individual impresses upon himself that he owes his own creative ability to G-d. Once this rationale is accepted, the student can be readily made to understand that the standard definitions of *melacha*, physical exertion, labor, work, etc., are totally misleading and incorrect. Question 2 brings home this point. Since halacha permits someone to carry a heavy table necessary for the Sabbath meal, or to carry a heavy set of books in order to study Torah, it is clear that physical exertion is not the decisive factor in determining whether a given act constitutes a prohibited *melacha*.

It has been my experience that even exceptional students who have completed the Yeshiva grade school display an abysmal lack of knowledge concerning the halacha of Shabbat. I have therefore included some material which defines the basic terms, *av melacha*, *tolada*. I think the teacher would be well-advised therefore to devote some time to the study of the thirty-nine *melachot*. The first eleven *melachot* are known as *sidura d'pat* and contain each of the steps necessary to bake bread. The *melachot* numbered twelve through twenty-four inclusive are each essential steps in making clothing. The *melachot* numbered twenty-five through thirty-one inclusive are necessary in making leather out of an animal skin. The remaining eight *melachot* do not fit into any broad categories. It should be stressed that the *kilkulim*, the destructive acts (nos. 24, 33, 35 and 37) are not considered *melachot* unless they are done for a constructive purpose. For example, if one were to tear a garment simply with the idea of destroying it, he would not be guilty of *melacha*. Of course, this would be prohibited by one of the Rabbinic *gezerot* (which will be discussed in lesson 12). If, however, one were to do precisely the same act with the constructive purpose of resewing it, it would be a *melacha*. As mentioned in the Student's Guide, this result fits in perfectly with the definition of *melacha* as constructive, creative human activity. A list of the thirty-nine *melachot follows*:

1. Plowing 2. Planting 3. Reaping 4. Making bundles 5. Threshing 6. Winnowing 7. Selecting 8. Sifting 9. Grinding 10. Kneading 11. Baking 12. Sheep shearing 13. Bleaching 14. Combing raw wool 15. Dyeing 16. Spinning 17, 18, 19. Weaving operations 20. Separating into threads 21. Tying a knot 22. Untying a knot 23. Sewing 24. Tearing 25. Trapping 26. Slaughtering 27. Skinning 28. Tanning 29. Making lines 30. Scraping 31. Cutting to shape 32. Writing 33. Erasing 34. Building 35. Demolishing 36. Kindling a fire 37. Extinguishing fire 38. Adding the final touches 39. Carrying from a private area into a public area or vice versa.

א) חורש ב) זורע ג) קוצר ד) מעמר ה) דש ו) זורה ז) בורר ח) מרקד ט) טוחן י) לש י"א) אופה י"ב) גוזז י"ג) מלבן י"ד) מנפץ ט"ו) צובע ט"ז) טווה י"ז) מיסך י"ח) עושה שתי בתי נירין י"ט) אורג כ) פוצע ב' חוטין כ"א) קושר כ"ב) מתיר כ"ג) תופר כ"ד) קורע כ"ה) צד כ"ו) שוחט כ"ז) מפשט כ"ח) מעבד כ"ט) משרטט ל) ממחק ל"א) מחתך ל"ב) כותב ל"ג) מוחק ל"ד) בונה ל"ה) סותר ל"ו) מבעיר ל"ז) מכבה ל"ח) מכה בפטיש ל"ט) הוצאה.

Since so many common machines depend upon electricity,

I have inserted question 5 to illustrate that putting on or off electricity is prohibited *mideoraitha*. Virtually all authorities agree that putting on electricity constitutes a *tolada* of "kindling a fire." (In fact, the Chazon Ish is of the opinion that it also constitutes "building.")

Lesson 10 begins with a conceptual analysis of the difference between *hotzaah* and the remaining *melachot*. The selection from Jeremiah also indicates that *hotzaah* is a special category. This leads to the problem posed in question 2, viz., since "carrying" involves no creative, physical change it must play some role other than acknowledging G-d as the master of the natural environment. Dayan Grunfeld ("The Shabbat," pp. 27-9) explains that "carrying" is the characteristic *melacha* by which man pursues and attains his ends in society. By ceasing from carrying we acknowledge G-d as the master of human society. The vast world of social organization needs such a *melacha* to express G-d's sovereignty over our social affairs.

Question 1 examines *hotzaah* in some detail. The *melacha* is made up of two distinct categories: (1) removing an object from a private domain (*r'shut hayachid*) for any purpose to a public domain (*r'shut harabim*) or vice versa; and (2) moving an object a distance of four cubits (approximately seven feet) within a public domain.

The *gezerot* called for by question 3 are: (1) carrying in a *carmelit* which although not a *r'shut harabim* can be confused with one, e.g., a park, an unfrequented place, a side street, etc.; (2) writing which is not permanent, e.g., on the frosted window-pane, or in sand; (3) tying a knot which is not permanent; however, a bow is permitted; (4) planting, or watering a flower-pot which is detached from the soil, or putting water into a vase of cut flowers; (5) the requirement of a "*blech*," a metal sheet covering the stove burners is an example of a *gezerah* to prevent the kindling of fire.

LESSON 11

THE SPIRIT OF SHABBAT

In this lesson I have attempted to evoke some feeling of the joyous atmosphere which fills the Jewish home on Sabbath. The verse selected from *Lecha Dodi* and the Talmudic passage (Shabbat 10b) refer to Shabbat as the "source of blessing" and a "precious gift." Certainly the proper Shabbat atmosphere qualifies on both counts. Our sages tell us that one who properly observes the Sabbath is given a *neshama yetera*, an additional soul, which makes possible the highest form of spiritual happiness and personal contentment.

The song *Lecha Dodi*, which ushers in the Sabbath, is most significant. If we attain that highest form of spiritual attainment which is only possible on the Sabbath, then we may call G-d, Himself, "my friend." The verse quoted in question 1 may be translated as follows: "Come let us go meet the Sabbath, for it is the source of blessings, sanctified from the very beginning, from days of antiquity, although the end of creation it was first in thought." Although Shabbat was the last day to be created, the Midrash tells us that weekdays were meant to usher in the Sabbath, just as the preparations of the wedding feast are meant to usher in the bride and groom. Shabbat dominates the week; the other days are merely preparations for it.

Question 2 merely states the obvious. Since Shabbat is a day of physical and spiritual contentment, it is not enough that we merely refrain from *melacha*. We must integrate *menucha* with *kedusha*. We must therefore be careful to refrain from activities which although not in themselves *melacha*, destroy the Sabbath atmosphere and mock the day's dignity and restfulness. Our sages refer to such behavior as *uvda d'chol*, common, every-day activity. Certainly, such activity as listening to a radio, or watching television, although not technically *melacha* (if put on by Sabbath clock), or engaging in athletic sports fall within this category. Similarly, worrying about one's business or financial affairs is prohibited. The verse in Isaiah (58:13) as interpreted by the Talmud (Shabbat 113a, b) indicates the length we must go to preserve Shabbat as a day apart from the weekdays.

‏"וקראת לשבת עונג לקדוש ה' מכבד וכבדתו מעשות דרכיך ממצוא חפצך ודבר דבר".

"And you shall honor it," that your Sabbath clothing should not be like your weekday clothing . . . *"Nor doing your own ways,"* that your walking on the Sabbath shall not be like your walking on weekdays. *"Nor finding your own affairs"*: Your affairs are forbidden, the affairs of Heaven are permitted. *"Nor speaking your own words,"* that your speech on Sabbat should not be like your speech on weekdays.

LESSON 12

GEZEROT: ERECTING FENCES AROUND
THE TORAH

Since reference was made to *gezerot* in the discussion of
the Sabbath, I feel this is an opportune place for a lesson
devoted to Rabbinic legislation. We are concerned with both
the Rabbinic authority and methodology in promulgating
new legislation. Future lessons will consider in detail the
concept of the written Torah and the oral tradition.

In the student's guide I have cited the appropriate Biblical verses which give the Rabbis authority to promulgate
legislation. The Rambam (*Mamrim* 1:2, and "*Sefer Hamitzvot*," *Shoresh* 1) specifically includes every Rabbinic *gezerah*
and *takanah* within the reach of *lo tasur*. As indicated in
question 3 we recite the standard *birkat hamitzva* prior to
the performance of a Rabbinic mitzva. This is based on the
Talmudic statement (Shabbat 23a) that a mitzva of the
Rabbis is considered to have been commanded by G-d. The
teacher might at this point wish to discuss the principle:

"יש כח ביד חכמים לעקור דבר מן התורה בשב ואל תעשה"

Based on this extension of Rabbinic protective legislative
authority, the "blowing of the Shofar" and the "taking of the
lulav" were prohibited on the Sabbath. The purpose of the

191

enactment was the fear that the common people might engage in *hotzaah*. The effect of the enactment was to nullify the Biblical imperative to perform the mitzva that day (blowing a shofar is not a *melacha*). (Cf. Rosh Hashana 29b, Succah 42b.)

Question 2 raises the problem of various schismatic groups in Jewish history, notably the Sadducees and the Kararites, who accepted the written Bible but denied the Rabbinic tradition and legislation. Although these groups flourished for a time, they eventually disappeared, either returning to the tradition or becoming absorbed into the gentile culture. The teacher, depending on both his personal inclination and the makeup of his class, might wish to analogize such groups with contemporary groups who deny traditional Rabbinic authority.

Finally, the methodology of *gezerot* is examined with specific reference to the Shabbat laws. Chazal have made two types of Shabbat *gezerot*. a) Acts which outwardly resemble a *melacha* and so might be confused with them. b) Acts which are linked with *melacha* by habit. Examples of the former are: tying a knot which does not amount to a permanent knot, *kilkulim* performed without any constructive purpose, carrying in a *carmelit*, writing which is not permanent, putting water into a vase of cut flowers, squeezing out the juice of fruits other than grapes and olives (that would be *deoraitha*), grating vegetables, combing one's hair, applying lipstick, or rouge, opening an umbrella. Examples of the second type are: doing something which is usually accompanied by writing, e.g., buying or selling, reading business correspondence, figuring complicated arithmetic problems, etc. Also, climbing a tree, riding a horse, smelling an edible fruit while it is on the tree, handling soaking clothes lest one come to wring it out, are all examples where by habit one may come to perform *melacha*. Perhaps the handling of a utensil ordinary used for *melacha* fits into this category (Cf. Rambam and Raavad, Shabbat 24:12, 13). Perhaps listening to radio or television which often leads to changing stations or readjusting the control also belongs here.

LESSONS 13, 14

ACHDUT HASHEM

In these two lessons the student is introduced to some
fundamental philosophic tenets of Judaism. It is our task
to make certain that these *yesodot* do not remain mere philosophic abstractions, but instead are made relevant with
their practical implications understood by the student. The
first two questions of Lesson 13, and Lesson 14, question 1
are designed to accomplish this purpose.

In the beginning of this lesson reference is made to the
Rambam's formulation of *Yesodei hayahadut* in his commentary on the first Mishna of *Chelek*. In later lessons dealing with specific principles, I have included in the Teacher's
Guide selections from this work both in the original and
translation which are suitable for class discussion. Certainly,
the student's attention should also be directed to the appropriate sections of the *Yigdal* and *Ani Maamin* prayers.

Since the affirmation of *Achdut Hashem* is given in the
Shema, the teacher may wish to mention some of Chazal's
comments on this posuk (*Devarim* 6:4). It is unnecessary to
detail here these interpretations other than to indicate that
the classical comment of the Siphre (partially quoted by
Rashi) attempting to reconcile the apparent contradiction
between *Hashem Elokeinu* and *Hashem Echad* is reproduced in full in the Teacher's Guide to Lesson 21.

194

Question 3 which poses the problem of reconciling G-D's incorporeality with the creation of man *b'zelem Elokim* is based upon the Rambam's discussion in *"Moreh Nevuchim"* (Part 1:1). "The term *zelem*, signifies the specific form, viz., that which constitutes the essence of a thing whereby the thing is what it is. In man the 'form' is that constituent which gives him human perception, and on account of this intellectual perception the term *zelem* is employed in the sentence 'In the *zelem* of G-D He created him' . . . I am also of the opinion that the reason why this term is used for idols may be found in the circumstance that they are worshipped on account of some idea represented by them, not on account of their figure and shape."

The central theme developed in Lesson 14 is the contemporary meaning of the prohibition against idol worship. Students must be made to recognize the eternal relevance of the Torah's precepts. The prohibition of idol worship is not limited to worship of wood or stone carvings but to placing one's faith and trust in any human creation. Rabbi E. Dressler in *"Michtav M'Eliyahu"* (Vol I, p. 175) uses the mitzva of *Yichud Hashem* to develop the theme that the emphasis within certain mitzvot often reflects changing cultural or intellectual conditions. In this manner he explains the shifting emphasis concerning *Yichud Hashem* and the prohibition against idol worship which can be found in Chazal. For example, the Rambam in Chapter One of *hilchot Avoda Zara* stresses that at times *Achdut Hashem* requires man to approach G-D directly rather than through intermediaries. This applies to an age which does not deny G-D but claims that the way to worship G-D is through intermediaries—an approach which the Rambam fears can easily lead to *Avoda Zara*. Similarly, in the Ramabam's own age, the popularity of Aristotelian philosophy necessitated a shift in focus reflected by the Rambam's insistence that philosophic speculation upon G-D's true nature is the way to fulfil the mitzva of *yichud Hashem.* Once again in our own day the focus of *Yichud Hashem* and idol worship has shifted in response to a new intellectual and cultural climate. I have tried to point out in the Student's Guide that placing absolute faith in science's ability to solve mankind's problems is nothing more than a sophisticated form of idol worship. This is not meant to suggest that religion and science should be viewed as natural antagonists, but rather that man should maintain a correct balance of priorities. Science must not become an end in itself, an object of worship. Question 4 suggests the great role science can play in deepening man's appreciation of the complexity and unity within creation.

Lesson 14 concludes with an examination of Biblical anthropomorphisms. The purpose of this discussion is to make clear that the use in the Torah of human, corporeal qualities in describing G-D is not meant as an accurate representation. The verses quoted are all examples of *Chazal's* maxim *"dibra Torah b'lashon bnei adam."* Maimonides in Part 1 of the *"Moreh Nevuchim"* devotes chapter 46 to this topic. The verses quoted and many other similar examples may be found in that chapter.

The problem of G-D's attributes is one which has produced much discussion in classical Jewish philosophy. I have not included any mention of it in the Student's Guide since it is of little practical relevance, and probably beyond the comprehension of most students. Nevertheness, if the teacher wishes to discuss this topic, this is the logical place. In the *"Moreh Nevuchim"* the Rambam devotes Part I, Chaps. 51-60, to his analysis of this topic. Essentially the Rambam is of the opinion that attributes attributed to G-D are to be understood in a negative sense. They do not tell us what G-D is, but what He is not. Thus, when we say that G-D is one, we do not really mean to imply that we know anything about G-D's true nature; we merely affirm that He is not a plurality of beings. Similarly, when we say that G-D is compassionate we refer to His acts, which if done by humans would be the product of compassion, and that He is not cruel. Any further discussion of this technical, philosophic topic is clearly beyond the scope and purpose of this volume.

LESSONS 15, 16

UNIVERSALISM AND GERUT

Lesson 15 concentrates on the universalism of Judaism, a universalism not shared by either of the western world's two other so-called great religions. Students rarely recognize this crucial difference between Judaism and both Christianity and Islam. The teacher would do well therefore to carefully point out this distinction with the specific examples enumerated in this lesson.

The universalism of Judaism is made obvious by the first two questions. The Torah does not begin with material specifically dealing with Jewish history, but with world history. Adam *harishon* is not the father of Israel but the father of all mankind. The first covenant between G-D and man is not with Israel, but with all mankind. The specific features of that covenant, the *shiva mitzvot bnei Noach*, are binding on all people for all time. An analysis of these laws reveals that they may be broken down, with some overlap, into three distinct categories of human conduct. *Avoda zara* and *birkat Hashem* are precepts which deal with religious behavior; *shfichat damim*, *gezel*, and *dinim* represent laws regulating legal behavior, while *giluy arayot* and *ever min hachay* deal with ethical behavior. In other words these seven precepts represent the standard required in the three major areas of human conduct. At the end of lesson 21 (Student's Guide) dealing with *am hanivchar*, we explore the obvious question of why only these seven mitzvot and not the whole of Torah apply to mankind universally. It would be best to defer discussion of this problem until then.

The universalism of Judaism as compared to the narrow parochialism of Christianity and Islam is most striking when we contrast each religion's respective attitude toward righteous people of other faiths. Only Judaism has a concept of *chasedei umot haolam*, whereby righteous behavior merits any individual a share in the world to come. Question 3 is designed to illustrate that both Christianity and Islam not only do not accept an analogous concept, but instead condemn to eternal damnation one who does not accept their religion. The Student's Guide contains a full discussion of how this universalism produces another great difference between Judaism and other religions, i.e., the contrast between the treatment of gentiles living in the Jewish state, and Jews living in *galut* in the non-Jewish state. The teacher should of course contrast the contemporary plight of Jews in Arab lands with that of Arabs living in Israel.

Lesson 16, question 2 points out that Judaism's universalism is an important factor in shaping our approach to *gerut*. Since Judaism recognizes G-D's covenant with the non-Jew, there is no need to attempt to convert others to our faith. The divine plan grants each individual, Jew and non-Jew alike, duties and responsibilities which if performed satisfactorily entitle that person to G-D's ultimate reward. The Student's Guide (based primarily on the Rambam's rulings in *Hilchot Issurei Biah* Chapters 13 and 14) contains a relatively complete description of how the halacha of *gerut* is designed to insure genuine conversion and to prevent conversion for insincere or extraneous purposes. Question 1 asks the student to identify some of the great figures of Jewish history who were *gerei tzedek*. The most striking example is that of Ruth for her descendants include David and Solomon —and therefore ultimately the Messiah who will be a descendant of David. Many of the great Tannaim were *gerim* or descendants of *gerim*. Actual converts include Shemayah, Avtalyon and Onkelos (*Gittin* 57b). The Tannaim Rabbi Akiva and Rabbi Meir were descendants of *gerim*. Question 4 raises the question of the status of the *ger tzedek*. Halacha of course recognizes no such thing as second-class citizenship. The *ger tzedek* is equated with the born Jew in all respects (*Shmot* 12:49, Rambam, *Issurei Biah* 12:17). In fact the following statement is typical of *Chazal's* attitude toward the righteous convert:

‏"חביב הגר לפני הקב"ה מן אותן אוכלסין שעמדו על הר סיני"‏

"The *ger* is more precious to the Holy One than the masses who stood at Mount Sinai."

At this point the teacher might very beneficially discuss the issue "Who is a Jew?" a question which during the past decade has periodically flared up and provoked the most extreme debate. Since the popular media, television and the magazines invariably pick up the discussion, and of course invariably from a perspective diametrically opposed to Torah Judaism, it is essential that the Torah position be explained and the flaws of those who would tamper with halacha be exposed.

In 1958 the Prime Minister of Israel addressed to Jewish scholars both in Israel and the diaspora a request for their opinions on this topic. The responses have been compiled in English by Boruch Litvin and Sidney Hoenig in a volume entitled "Jewish Identity: Modern Responsa and Opinions" (New York, 1965). Besides many Israeli *gedolim* who answered, responses were received from many American scholars including Rav Aharon Kotler z.l., Rav Menachem Mendel

Schneerson, the Lubavitcher Rebbe, and Rav J. B. Solo-
veichik.

The crucial issue is whether Jewish nationality can be
divorced from Jewish religion. A recent decision of the Israeli
Supreme Court made such a decision when it recognized the
right of an individual not born a Jew to register as a Jew by
nationality merely by declaring that he considers himself
Jewish. The Israeli government recognized the danger to
Jewish unity inherent in the Court's decision and passed
legislation superseding and overruling the court's decision.
The statute enacted by the Kenesset recognized that no
distinction could be made between Jewish nationality and
Jewish religion and therefore required that in order to be
registered as a Jewish national the applicant must have
either been born a Jew, i.e., the child of a Jewish mother or
have converted to Judaism. Nevertheless, the Kenesset legislation is seriously deficient from a Torah perspective since
it does not specifically require that the conversion be done
according to halacha. The following response of Rav Aharon
Kotler z.l. ("Jewish Identity" p. 105) is a clear and forthright
statement of our position. "There is no difference what-
soever between the terms 'religion' and 'nationality' because such a distinction does not exist in Jewry. It has no
halachic or practical meaning . . . As for national unity, it is
perfectly clear that only the Torah unites Israel distinguishing
it from all other nations and makes it one entity in the
world."

The Mishna in *Kiddushim* (65b) based upon the posuk
in *Devarim* (7:13) clearly establishes that the offspring of a
Jewish father and a non-Jewish mother is not a Jew. The
principle is also evident in Ezra (10:2, 3) where the Jews
who had taken an oath to send away their gentile wives from
the Jewish community, also sent away their children.
Although it is usually neither necessary nor proper to offer

justifications for a particular Biblical rule, should the question arise as to why the child's status depends upon the mother, the teacher can point out that children's basic, formative education is usually provided by the mother.

„כל עבד עברי אסור לישראל שקנהו להעבידו בדברים כוזים שהם
מיוחדים לעשות העבדים כגון שיוליך אחריו כליו לבית המרחץ או יחלוץ
מנעליו שנאמר 'לא תעבוד בו עבודת עבד' אינו נוהג בו אלא כשכיר
שנאמר 'כתושב יהיה עמך'... בד"א בעבד עברי מפני שנפשו שפלה
במכירה אבל ישראל שלא נמכר מותר להשתמש בו כעבד שהרי אינו
עושה מלאכה זו אלא ברצונו ומדעת עצמו".

Question 5 raises the problem of an *eved ivri* who has the
responsibility of supporting a family. The Rambam in
Avadim (3:1, 2) based on various Talmudic *drashot*, explains that the master is required to provide support for the
eved's wife and children, even though they are not in his
service and remain *bnei chorin*. This ruling applies both if the
eved married before or during his period of *avdut*.

Lesson 18 examines the institution of *eved cannani*. The
lesson begins with a discussion of the various methods employed by halacha to insure the *eved's* physical well-being.
Question 1 asks the student to identify safeguards erected
by the Torah to prevent the possibility of physical beatings
so common in the ordinary master-slave relationship. The
Torah (*Shmot* 21:26, 27) specifically mentions that if the
adon smites the *eved's* eye or tooth, he must be freed. The
Talmud (*Kiddushin* 24a) explains that *shen v'ayin* are representative of the other limbs and the rule applies if any
one of twenty-four limbs is smitten. Moreover, if the *adon*
beats the *eved* so severely as to cause death, the *adon* is
considered an ordinary murderer and is liable for the death
penalty ("*Moreh Nevuchim*" 3:39).

Question 2 is based on the selection from the "*Moreh
Nevuchim*" (*ibid.*) where the Rambam quotes the following
verse (*Devarim* 23:17): "He shall dwell with you in the
place which he chooses of your gates which he likes best;
you shall not oppress him." The Rambam generalizes from

these verses dealing with the escaping *eved* the requirement to assist all those who seek our help. He explains that it is simple logic (*kal vachomer*) to apply this principle not only to the *eved* but to all who need aid. Nevertheless the Rambam qualifies the rule; it does not apply to sinners who attempt to avoid justice.

The remainder of the lesson concentrates on the unique status of the *eved cannani*. His is a transitional phase, from that of non-Jew to that of *ger tzedek*. Immediately upon purchase the *eved* is asked whether he wishes to accept the mitzvot which apply to an *eved cannani*, i.e., all the negative prohibitions (*lavim*) and positive commandments which are not dependent upon time (*mitzvot aseh sheein hazaman gerama*). If he is willing, the same procedure which we saw in the lesson devoted to *gerut* is followed. The *eved* is taught the essential principles of Judaism and various mitzvot, followed by *milah* and *tevilla* (Rambam, *Hilchot Issurei Biah* 14:9). If the *eved* refuses to accept these responsibilities, a maximum period of one year is provided wherein he may change his mind. If he remains steadfast in his refusal, he must be resold to a non-Jew. Question 3 draws the obvious conclusion that the *eved's* unique status necessarily influences the relationship with his *adon*. The *adon* is no ordinary master; he has the responsibility to make certain that his *eved* is adequately prepared to become a full-fledged Jew.

LESSONS 19, 20

AM HANIVCHAR

Few principles of Judiasm are as little known or stressed as *am hanivchar*. This concept, so crucial to Judiasm, is one which the contemporary student nurtured on democratic ideas finds difficult to accept. In these two lessons the fact of *am hanivchar* is considered and historical proofs are adduced thereto. The following lesson focuses attention on what *am hanivchar* entails; rights and duties, positives and negatives which follow from Israel's selection are examined.

I think it best to begin the lesson with an examination of the unique character of Jewish history. In the Student's Guide stress is placed on Israel's continuity, the very fact of Jewish existence, despite the numerous attempts throughout history to obliterate that identity. The student should be made to realize that no other ancient people retain their national identity into the modern era. Neither modern Italy, nor Greece, nor Egypt nor any other nation shares a common culture with their ancestors of thousands of years ago. The situation of Israel should be contrasted with the other nations. We alone share a common heritage with our forefathers. We speak a common language, study the same Torah, and perform the same mitzvot.

Although this alone would be sufficient to establish the

uniqueness of Israel, the teacher may develop this theme with many examples from world and Jewish history. In order to place the discussion in its proper perspective, I have indicated in the Student's Guide that the central role played by Jews in the world's history cannot be attributed to great numbers—in Biblical days as well as in our own. Furthermore, selection is not solely reflected by triumph; disaster and calamity equally reflect our uniqueness. The concerted effort by nation after nation in ancient as well as modern times to oppress and destroy the Jewish people is painful but eloquent testimony that the world recognizes that we are different. Ancient Greece and Rome, medieval Spain and England, modern Germany and Russia have each attempted to crush either physically or spiritually the Jewish people. It is a historical fact that after every such attempt we have arisen stronger and more dedicated to our faith.

The remarkable Jewish contributions in so many diverse areas throughout history are also evidence of the unique character of our people. The student should recognize that one's perception of history is necessarily dependent upon the bias of the historical authors he has read. Since the textbooks used by many students, either consciously or unconsciously, play down Jewish contributions even is secular history, the teacher might find it advisable to mention some of these little known contributions. For example, ancient Rome's great legacy to modern civilization is its legal system which serves as the basis for most of the legal system of the non-English speaking world. Little mention is made of the great influence of Jewish law in shaping that law. Similarly, Jewish merchants and traders were in great measure responsible for the rebirth of European trade and commerce after the dark ages.

Certainly, however, the concept of *am hanivchar* can be made most meaningful if we focus on contemporary history.

In the two lessons dealing with miracles (6 and 7), the point was made that taken in their totality the events in Jewish history of the past three decades defy any natural explanation and compel the conclusion of G-d's intervention in the affairs of His *am hanivchar*. The teacher would do well at this point to reinforce that conclusion. This is also an excellent opportunity to discuss the plight of our Russian brethren. After the Jews no people suffered as much as the Russians at the hands of the Nazis. Simple logic dictates that shared, common suffering would deter Russia from repeating such inhuman crimes on the Jews and yet Russia has embarked on just such a course of conduct.

Lesson 19 concludes and lesson 20 begins with the Rambam's analysis (*Avodat Cochavim* 1:1-3) of the history of the period following the flood. The Rambam's purpose in this extended discussion is to make clear the greatness and uniqueness of our father Abraham so that his selection as the father of *am hanivchar* can be readily understood. Question 3 of lesson 19 dealing with the construction of *migdal Bavel* is intended to delineate the religious climate which was then current. The quoted verse (*Bereshit* 11:4): "And they say, come and we will build for us a city and a tower, whose head may reach unto heaven, so that we will make for ourselves a name . . ." indicates the nature of the generation's sin. Mankind gathered in unison to wage battle against G-d. The tower extending to heaven symbolizes this rebellion and man's futile attempt at self-deification.

Question 4 discusses the legends of Babylonia and other ancient people, e.g., the epic of Gilgamesh, which in many respects are markedly similar to the Biblical account of the flood and the story of *migdal Bavel*. It is obvious that these tales retain the core of historical fact as described in the Torah, although they are embellished with superstitions and legends. The existence of such legends is of course proof of the historical authenticity of the Biblical stories. In fact within the past year (1970) discoveries of wood at Ararat in Turkey have convinced archaeologists that they have found remnants of Noah's ark.

Lesson 20 begins with the Rambam's description (*Avodat Cochavim* 1:3) of the intellectual greatness and spiritual grandeur of Avraham. The teacher should make clear Avraham's uniqueness as compared with other righteous men. Not only did he discover without the aid of tradition or teachers the truth of *achdut Hashem* and the implications which necessarily follow, but also he did not keep the discovery to himself or his family. Instead he dedicated himself to spreading the truth of G-d and the need to serve Him to all those he could influence. This is the answer to question 1. The covenant with Abraham was not the result of chance. G-d does not enter into an eternal covenant with every righteous man, only with an Abraham. We can only surmise from the silence of the Torah that Abraham's followers and their descendants eventually disappeared as a separate, identifiable group. This leads directly to question 2 and the discussion thereon which analyzes why *zera Avraham* merited becoming G-D's chosen people. The lesson concludes with an analysis of why G-d established His Torah for a particular people rather than for mankind universally. This topic is developed in the next lesson.

Relevant selections from the Rambam's discussion (*ibid.*) follow:

„והוא קטן והתחיל לחשוב ביום ובלילה והיה תמיה היאך אפשר שיהיה הגלגל הזה נוהג תמיד ולא יהיה לו מנהיג ומי יסבב אותו... ולא היה לו מלמד ולא מודיע דבר אלא מושקע באור כשדים בין עובדי כוכבים... ובן ארבעים שנה הכיר אברהם את בוראו [עיין כסף משנה שם 'כשהיה בן ארבעים השלים להכירו' אבל התחיל לחשוב ולהכירו כשהיה בן שלש שנים] כיון שהכיר וידע התחיל להשיב תשובות על בני אור כשדים ולערוך דין עמהם ולומר שאין זו דרך אמת שאתם הולכים בה ושיבר

הצלמים והתחיל להודיע לעם שאין ראוי לעבוד אלא לאלוה העולם...
והיה מהלך וקורא ומקבץ העם מעיר לעיר וממלכה לממלכה עד שהגיע
לארץ כנען... וכיון שהיו העם מתקבצין אליו ושואלין לו על דבריו
היה מודיע לכל אחד ואחד כפי דעתו עד שיחזירהו לדרך האמת עד
שנתקבצו אליו אלפים ורבבות והם אנשי בית אברהם ושתל בלבם העיקר
הגדול הזה וחבר בו ספרים והודיעו ליצחק בנו וישב יצחק מלמד ומזהיר
ויצחק הודיע ליעקב...״

THE MISSION OF ISRAEL

In this lesson we examine G-d's purpose in selecting an *am hanivchar*. The *Siphre* on the sentence of *Shema Yisroel* (*Devarim* 6:4) attempts to reconcile the apparent contradiction between "*Hashem Elokeinu*"—the national, and "*Hashem echad*"—the universal, in two ways. These two answers in essence comprise the theme of this lesson.

„ 'ה' אלקינו' — למה נאמר והלה כבר נאמר 'ה' אחד' ומה ת"ל אלקינו
עלינו הוחל שמו ביותר... דבר אחר 'ה' אלקינו' בעולם הזה 'ה' אחד'
בעולם הבא וכה"א (זכריה ח') 'והיה ה' למלך על כל הארץ ביום ההוא
יהיה ה' אחד ושמו אחד"

The first answer suggested by the *Siphre* "upon us His name rests" means that it is Israel which introduced to the world the idea of one G-d. It is our task through our unique way of life to bring all mankind to a realization and acknowledgement of the one G-d. When this is accomplished mankind will enter the Messianic era which the *Siphre* calls *olam haba*.

In the Student's Guide the twin functions of *goy kadosh* and *mamlechet Cohanim* are developed in some detail. The teacher in his discussion of *kadosh* would be well advised to develop the following idea. *Kadosh* requires *havdala*, separation. Our students should be impressed with the practical significance of this concept. Slavish adherence to the latest modes of dress or hair style certainly do not reflect the proper behavior of a member of *am kadosh*. Obviously this does not mean that we are "required" to adopt a unique style of dress, although certainly if one does so *tova alav bracha*. There is a *kav hayashar*, a middle road, in this as in all other areas of life. It is sufficient if our clothing conforms to the halachic standards of *tznuit*. Closely connected to this theme is the famous comment of the Ramban on the Biblical command of *kedoshim tihyu* (*Vayikra* 19:2):

" 'קדושים תהיו' — פרושים תהיו... והענין כי התורה הזהירה בעריות
ובמאכלים האסורים והתירה הביאה איש באשתו ואכילת בשר ויין א״כ
ימצא בעל התאוה מקום... והנה יהיה נבל ברשות התורה לפיכך בא
הכתוב אחרי שפרט האיסורים שאסר אותם לגמרי וצוה בדבר כללי שנהיה
פרושים מן המותרות."

An individual may violate no specific prohibitions of the Torah and yet his behavior may be so abhorrent that he is classified as a *"naval birshut hatorah,"* a vile, disgraceful person. One must not give free rein to his *taavot*, his physical passions and desires—moderation must be the controlling principle.

The answer to question 5, i.e., why *Keriyat Shema* of both *Shachrit* and *Arvit* is preceded by the *bracha* of Israel's selection, is evident after the discussion in this lesson. *Keriyat Shema* is *kabbalat ol malchut shamayim*, Israel's acceptance of G-d's sovereignity and its divine mission to make *Hashem Echad* acknowledged throughout all mankind. Certainly the appropriate place for the blessing establishing this mission is immediately prior to *kabbalat ol malchut shamayim*.

Question 4 points out that Cohanim, in fact all *shevet Levi*, were not at all analogous to the priestly class of other religions. As the Rambam stresses (*Shmita V'yovel* 13:12) *shevet Levi* did not share in *chalukat Eretz Yisroel,* the division of the land of Israel, nor did they attempt to amass personal wealth. They were not set aside as a privileged social class but were *"cheil Hashem,"* G-d's warriors. Theirs was a two-fold function — to serve G-d, in the Temple and as the teachers of Israel.

„ולמה לא זכה לוי בנחלת ארץ ישראל ובביזתה עם אחיו מפני שהובדל
לעבוד את ה׳ לשרתו ולהורות דרכיו הישרים ומשפטיו הצדיקים לרבים
שנאמר ׳יורו משפטיך ליעקב ותורתך לישראל לפיכך הובדלו מדרכי
העולם לא עורכין מלחמה כשאר ישראל ולא נוחלין ולא זוכין לעצמן
בכח גופן אלא הם חיל השם.״

LESSON 22

TEFILLA: PRAYER

We begin our discussion of prayer with an analysis of its central role in impressing upon man G-d's concern with the affairs of each individual human being. The student should realize both intellectually and emotionally that when he recites *Shmoneh Esreh* he not only is fulfilling a religious obligation, but is truly engaging in dialogue with G-d. The practical implications of this experience should be stressed. A *mithpallel* must approach prayer in a manner befitting an encounter with the King of kings. The concentration necessary for *kavanah*, a meaningful prayer-dialogue with God, is incompatible with certain mental states. One does not pray in the heat of anger or in the midst of frivolity. The *mithpallel* should also be physically fit for prayer. The teacher should develop the ramifications which follow—both in terms of personal cleanliness and appropriate attire.

Question 2 points out that in fact the *Shmoneh Esreh* we recite today contains nineteen separate blessings. *Anshei Knesset Hagdolah* after the destruction of the first *Bet Hamikdash* originally established *shmoneh esreh* or eighteen benedictions and this has remained the name for the *Amida*. However, in the period following the destruction of the Second Temple, various schismatic groups arose and attempted to corrupt the traditional Jewish teaching. *Chazal* created a special *bracha*, *V'lamalshinim*, in response to these groups. The *bracha* calls for Divine condemnation of all those who would divide and thus destroy, either spiritually or physically, the people of Israel.

The teacher might at this point wish to discuss the famous argument of Maimonides and Nachmanides as to whether daily prayer is a mitzva *deoraitha*, a Biblical command. In the Student's Guide I have quoted in translation the Rambam's ruling (*Tefilla* 1:1) that daily prayer is one of the 613 mitzvot. The Ramban disagrees ("*Sefer Hamitzvot*," Mitzva 5) claiming that daily prayer is not a mitzva *deoraitha*. Rabbi Yechiel Michel Epstein in "*Aruch Hashulchan*" (89:6) quoted below offers an important insight into *tefilla* in his explanation of the Ramban's opinion. *Tefilla* is not counted as one of the *taryag* mitzvot because it is fundamental and axiomatic to Judaism. Similarly, many commentators (e.g., the author of *Baal Halachot Gedolot*) do not count *Anochi Hashem Elokecha*, the first of the Ten Commandments, which requires belief in G-d, as one of the *minyan hamitzvot* since this belief is the *yesod* or axiom from which all other mitzvot are derived. The statement of Rabbi Epstein follows:

„ונראה לע"ד לפי הרמב"ן שאינה נחשבת בין פרטי המצות לפי שהוא
גבוה מעל גבוה שהתפלה הרי כעומד לפני המלך ומדבר עמו פנים בפנים
כביכול ולכן הוא דוקא מעומד באימה ויראה... ענין התפלה אינה נכנסת
בפרטי המצות מפני שהתפלה היא ענין כללי".

LESSONS 23, 24

THE STRUCTURE OF SHMONEH ESREH

The first major topic discussed in these lessons is the crucial question posed at the conclusion of lesson 22, i.e., why should prayer be required at fixed times rather than result solely out of the individual's subjective inspiration. It was indicated in the Student's Guide that inspiration is too rare for most men to realistically serve as the sole factor in determining when men should pray. Nevertheless, as we shall see, the halachic structure is finely balanced so as to allow wide scope to the subjective, spontaneous impulses of the individual.

Lesson 23 begins with the famous Talmudic discussion (*Berakot* 26b) which explains that *Anshei Knesset Hagdolah* established the three daily prayers either to commemorate the *tefillot* recited by our *avot* or to substitute for the *korbanot* in the Temple. The novel approach advanced by the author of the "Kuzari" (part 3:5) which follows in translation, should be stressed as an example of the balance which Judaism establishes between the physical and spiritual parts of man. "Those three times of daily prayer are the fruit of his day and night . . . All this stands in the same relation to the soul as food to the human body. Prayer is for his soul what nourishment is for his body. The blessing of one prayer

217

lasts until the time of the next, just as the strength derived from the morning meal lasts until supper."

Questions 3 and 4 and the discussion thereon indicate that the text of *tefilla* and other prayers was established through the medium of prophecy. This explains why Jews throughout the ages have been so careful to preserve intact the exact text. The Rambam (*Berakot* 1:5) makes this clear.

„ונוסח כל הברכות עזרא ובית דינו תקנום ואין ראוי לשנותם ולא להוסיף
על אחת מהם ולא לגרוע ממנה. וכל המשנה ממטבע שטבעו חכמים
בברכות אינו אלא טועה".

"The text of all the *brachot* were established by Ezra and his Beth Din. It is not proper to change them, neither to add nor subtract from any of them. Any one who changes the text of *Berakot* coined by the *Chachamim* is in error."

The Gemara (*Berakot* 33a) answers question 4. Besides the *tefillot*, *Anshei Knesset Hagdolah* also established the text of *brachot*, and the *kiddushim* and *havadalot* recited on the Sabbath and *Yom Tovim*.

In the remainder of lesson 23 and lesson 24, I have concentrated on the text of *Shmoneh Esreh* since it is the key of all our prayers. It is hoped that an appreciation and understanding of the structure of the *Shmoneh Esreh* will enable the student to pray more meaningfully. The discussion commences with the Rambam's analysis of the three separate categories of blessings found in *Shmoneh Esreh*. The halachic significance of these different sections called for by question 6 is found in *Berakot* (34a) which treats *shevach* and *hodaah* as indissoluble units. If a *mithpallel* becomes aware of an error made in one of the *shevach brachot*, he must return to the start of *Shmoneh Esreh* even though the first blessing was recited properly. The same ruling applies to the *hodaah*

section. If an error has been made, the *mithpallel* must return
to *Avoda*, the first of these blessings.

Question 4 of lesson 24 introduces an extremely important and often overlooked aspect of prayer. Halacha, as
we mentioned before, does not eliminate the subjective
element in prayer. The Talmud (*Berakot* 21a) quotes Rav
Yochanan who urged prayer the whole day. *Rishonim* explain that this refers to *tefillot nedava*, the individual's free-
will, spontaneous prayer which may be recited if it contains
some *chiddush*, an individual, personal element to distinguish
it from the ordinary *tefillot chova* (See Rambam, *Tefilla* 1:9,
and *Shulchan Aruch, Orach Hayim* 107:2, 3). Although
today we do not recite *tefillot nedava* due to the difficulty of
achieving genuine *kavanah*, halacha provides the opportunity
for individual expression even within *tefillot chova*. The
Gemara (*Avoda Zara* 8a) states:

„אמר רב יהודה משמיה דרב אע״פ שאמרו שואל אדם צרכיו בשומע
תפלה אבל אם בא לומר בסוף כל ברכה וברכה מעין כל ברכה וברכה
אומר אמר רב חייא בר אשי אמר רב אע״פ שאמרו שואל אדם צרכיו
בשומע תפלה אם יש לו חולה בתוך ביתו אומר בברכת חולים ואם צריך
לפרנסה אומר בברכת השנים״.

"Said Rav Yehudah in the name of Rav: Even though it
was said that one may pray for his private needs within the
benediction 'Who heareth prayer', nevertheless, if he is so
disposed he may at the end of the blessing supplement with
personal requests relevant to the subject matter of each
particular blessing. So also said R. Hiya b. Ashi in the name
of Rav: Even though it was said that one may pray for his
private needs within '*Shomea Tefilla*' still if one has a sick
person at home, he may offer a prayer at the blessing for
the sick; or if he is in want of sustenance, he may offer a
special prayer within the blessing for prosperous years." The
rule requires the personal insertion to be relevant to the

subject matter of the particular *bracha*. Thus in the *bracha* for the sick it is customary to insert a petition for the good health of one who is ill, even mentioning his name (*Mogen Avraham, Orach Hayim* 119:1). Similarly, during the recent Six-Day War, it would have certainly been proper for an individual *mithpallel* to have inserted his own prayer for the State of Israel in the *bracha Boneh Yerushalayim*. The blessing *Shomea Tefilla* is general, all-encompassing, and therefore any request can properly be inserted therein. It should be stressed that in each of the above instances and in similar insertions in any of the other *bakasha brachot* the option of supplementing the standardized text, and the wording of the particular insertion are left entirely to the *mithpallel*.

LESSON 25

DIVINE REVELATION AT SINAI

This lesson is the first of a series devoted to the source and nature of both Torah *she-bektav* and Torah *she-beal peh*. It is essential that such fundamental concepts as *maamad har Sinai*, Torah *min hashamayim* and particularly the masorah of Torah *she-beal peh* are developed and clarified for the student. Too often even the good student has only a vague and general idea of these *ikkarei hayahadut*.

At the beginning of this lesson reference is made to the statement of *Chazal* quoted by Rashi (*Shmot* 19:19) that only the first two commandments were heard from G-d's mouth. There are two reasons for the inclusion of this discussion. Besides the obvious desire for an accurate description of *maamad har Sinai*, there is a more significant justification. Certainly the literal text of Torah *she-bektav* does not necessitate such an interpretation. The teacher, therefore, has an opportunity at the very outset of the discussion to make the point that Torah *she bektav* can be accurately understood only in accordance with the traditional interpretation of *Chazal*.

The first two questions and the discussion thereon are suggested by the Rambam's (*Yesodei Hatorah* 8:1) analysis of *maamad har Sinai* which follows:

„משה רבינו לא האמינו בו ישראל מפני האותות שעשה. שהמאמין על
פי האותות יש בלבו דופי שאפשר שיעשה האות בלט וכשוף. אלא כל
האותות שעשה משה במדבר לפי הצורך עשאם. לא להביא ראיה על
הנבואה. היה צריך להשקיע את המצריים קרע את הים והצלילן בתוכו.
צרכנו למזון הוריד לנו את המן. צמאו בקע להן את האבן. כפרו בו עדת
קרח בלעה אותן הארץ. וכן שאר כל האותות. ובמה האמינו בו במעמד
הר סיני שעינינו ראו ולא זר ואזנינו שמעו ולא אחר האש והקולות
והלפידים והוא נגש אל הערפל והקול מדבר אליו ואנו שומעים משה משה
לך אמור להם כך וכך. וכן הוא אומר 'פנים בפנים דבר ה' עמכם'. ונאמר
'לא את אבותינו כרת ה' את הברית הזאת'. ומנין שמעמד הר סיני לבדו
היא הראיה לנבואתו שהיא אמת שאין בו דופי שנאמר 'הנה אנכי בא
אליך בעב הענן בעבור ישמע העם בדברי עמך וגם בך יאמינו לעולם',
מכלל שקודם דבר זה לא האמינו בו נאמנות שהיא עומדת לעולם אלא
נאמנות שיש אחריה הרהור ומחשבה".

In the Student's Guide two related functions are ascribed
to Divine Revelation. First, the great spiritual shock felt
by *Am Yisroel* at Sinai made *hakarat Hashem* and *Yirat
Hashem* an integral part of the Jewish psyche to be transmitted from parent to child throughout the generations.
Second, *maamad har Sinai* established firmly the people's
absolute faith in Moshe and in the prophets who succeeded
him. In this connection it would be appropriate to cite the
comment of Rashi on the phrase *"v'gam becha yaaminu
l'olam"* from the verse quoted in the Student's Guide (*Shmot*
19:9):

„גם בנביאים הבאים אחריך".

Once the two purposes of Sinaitic Revelation are understood, the answer to question 3 is obvious. *Devarim* (5:19-30)
details the fear felt by Israel at Sinai and their request to
Moshe that he act as G-d's intermediary in transmitting the
rest of Torah. Spiritual shock is not enhanced by an extended
revelation. Furthermore, the second great purpose, i.e., establishing Israel's absolute trust in Moshe, is cemented by
Moshe's role in transmitting the rest of Torah to Israel.

The final two questions contrast the public character of *maamad har Sinai* and the miracles of the Exodus from Egypt with the claimed private revelation of other religions. Virtually all classical Jewish philosophers stress that it would be impossible for a belief in public revelation to arise and pass unchallenged unless it was rooted in historical fact. Conversely, no other religion dares make claim of a public revelation.

LESSONS 26, 27

THE TORAH IS DIVINE AND UNCHANGING

It is no exaggeration that after the belief in G-d himself the single most fundamental principle is the belief in *Torah min hashamayim* and its corrolary the immutability of Torah. It is not surprising therefore to find that Rav Yosef Albo who in his "*Sefer Haikkarim*" limits the *ikkarim* to three, includes among them the belief in *Torah min hashamayim*. It is particularly important in our own age where so much of secular "Biblical scholarship" is devoted to the pernicious theories of Biblical criticism attempting to show the human origin of the Bible that this *ikkar* be stressed to the extent which it deserves. Let us not delude ourselves. Many of our students will in the future be exposed to Biblical criticism and it is our responsibility to inculcate within them a firm acceptance of *Torah min hashamayim* which will enable them to reject any contrary notions.

Certainly the most logical starting point is the Rambam's formulation of the eighth principle in his Commentary on the first Mishna of the tenth chapter of *Sanhedrin*.

„היסוד השמיני היות התורה מן השמים והוא שנאמין כי כל התורה הזאת הנתונה ע״י משה רבינו ע״ה שהיא כולה מפי הגבורה כלומר שהגיעה אליו כולה מאת ה׳ יתברך בענין שנקרא על דרך השאלה דבור ואין יודע היאך הגיע אלא הוא משה ע״ה שהגיע לו וכי הוא היה כמו סופר שקוראין לו והוא כותב כל מאורעות הימים הספורים והמצות ולפיכך נקרא מחוקק

ואין הפרש בין 'ובני חם כוש ומצרים' 'ושם אשתו מהטבאל' 'תמנע היתה
פגלש' ובין 'אנכי ה' אלקיך' 'ושמע ישראל' כי הכל מפי הגבורה והכל
תורת ה' תמימה טהורה וקדושה אמת וזה שאומר שכמו אלה הפסוקים
והספורים משה ספרם מדעתו הנה הוא אצל חכמינו ונביאינו כופר ומגלה
פנים יותר מכל הכופרים לפי שחשב שיש בתורה לב וקליפה ושאלה
דברי הימים והספורים אין תועלת בהם ושהם מאת משה רבינו ע"ה וזה
ענין אין תורה מן השמים אמרו חכמים ז"ל 'הוא המאמין שכל התורה
מפי הגבורה חוץ מן הפסוק זה שלא אמר הקב"ה אלא משה מפי עצמו..."

"The eighth principle of faith is that the Torah has been revealed from heaven. This requires our belief that the whole of this Torah which was given through Moshe Rabbeinu is totally from the mouth of G-d, i.e., that the whole of Torah came to him from G-d in a manner which is metaphorically called speaking, but the real nature of that communication is unknown except to Moshe to whom it came. And he [Moshe] was like a scribe to whom it was dictated and he wrote all the histories, the narratives and the mitzvot. Therefore, he is called *mechokek*, copyist. There is no difference between verses like 'And the sons of Ham were Cush and Mizraim' (*Bereshit* 10:6) or 'And his wife's name was Mehetabel' (*Bereshit* 36:39), or 'And Timna was a concubine' (*Bereshit* 26:12), and verses like 'I am the Lord your G-d' (*Shmot* 20: 2) and, 'Hear, O Israel' (*Devarim* 6:4). They are all of divine origin and all belong to 'the law of G-d which is perfect, pure, holy, and true.' One who says that such sentences and narratives were composed by Moses is considered by our Rabbis and prophets as the greatest of infidels and renegades since he implies that the Torah contains a kernel and a husk, and that these histories and anecdotes have no value and emanate from Moses. This is the significance of the expression 'The Torah does no come from heaven,' which say the Rabbis (*Sanhedrin* 99a), is the remark of one who believes that all of Torah is of divine origin except for one verse which he says was not spoken by G-d but by Moses himself.''

Questions 1 and 2 of lesson 26 deal with famous Talmudic discussions concerning problems raised in connection with the writing of *Torah she-bektav*. The relevant Talmudic sources are cited in the Student's Guide and additional material may be found in the Ramban's Introduction to his Commentary on *Chumash*.

Question 3 indicates that the halachic practice reflects the unique character of the final eight sentences. In *Orach Hayim* (428:7) the *Shulchan Aruch* based on *Menachot* (30a) rules that the final eight verses must be read as a unit by one *oleh*, even though ordinarily no more than three verses are required for any individual *aliyah*.

Question 4 points out that the Gemara ordinarily introduces a Biblical quotation with the phrase *"Rachmana amar,"* the "Compassionate one says." It goes without saying that a *posuk* is always ascribed to G-d. The remainder of question 4 draws the student's attention to the relevant passages in *Yigdal* and *Ani Maamin* to the principle of *Torah min hashamayim*. The reference to Moshe in *Yigdal* as *nehman beto* is based on *Bamidbar* (12:7).

Question 3 of lesson 27 asks the student to distinguish between two separate themes which make up the Rambam's ninth article of faith, i.e., the Torah is unchanging. The immutability of Torah has practical implications both externally, i.e., vis-a-vis other religions and internally, within Judaism. Externally, it affirms that Judaism is an eternal faith which will never be superseded by any other religion. Within Judaism, it affirms that the laws of Torah are eternal; they are not subject to change with the passage of time. This of course is the point of the verse from *Devarim* (13:1) quoted in question 5, and is the basis for the test of the *navi sheker*.

Question 6 asks the student for the contradiction implicit in Christian and Moslem theology. Both of these religions accept the truth of Sinaitic Revelation. However, each claims that this Revelation was superseded by a later revelation. The logical inconsistency is apparent; Sinaitic Revelation clearly states that its percepts are *chukot olam*, eternal, never to be abolished.

LESSONS 28, 29

TORAH SHE-BEAL PEH

It is my experience that many students do not have an adequate understanding of what is meant by Torah *she-beal peh*. Needless to say the deleterious effect on both their Talmudic studies and *hashkafa* cannot be overestimated. The series of lessons devoted to this topic is designed to accomplish two things: 1) to impress upon the student the inestimable role played by the oral tradition in arriving at the true meaning of G-d's law, 2) to delineate the various categories of Torah *she-beal peh* so that the student's Talmudic study will become more meaningful.

We begin Lesson 28 with a discussion of the source of Torah *she-beal peh*. It is imperative that the student recognize that Torah *min hashamayim* applies equally to the oral tradition. The classic Rabbinic statement is the first sentence in *Avot*:

„משה קבל תורה מסיני ומסרה ליהושע...".

It is clear that "Torah" refers both to Torah *bektav* and *beal peh*. The Rambam's formulation of the eighth principle of faith quoted in the preceding Teacher's Guide concludes with the following observation:

„וכמו כן פירש התורה המקובל גם כן מפי הגבורה וזה שאנו עושים היום מתבנית הסוכה ולולב ושופר וציצית ותפילין וזולתם היא בעצמו

228

התבנית אשר אמר השם יתברך למשה והוא אמר לנו והוא נאמן בשליחותו
והמאמר המורה על היסוד הזה הוא מה שנאמר 'ויאמר משה בזאת תדעון
כי ה' שלחני לעשות כל המעשים האלה כי לא מלבי".

"The Traditional interpretation of the Torah is likewise of divine origin. That which we know today of the nature of Succah, lulav, shofar, tzitzit, tefillin is exactly the same as which G-d told Moshe, and which he told us, and he was faithful in his mission. The verse which indicates this principle is (*Bamidbar* 16:28) 'And Moses said, hereby you shall know that G-d sent me to do all these works, for they are not of my own heart'."

Questions 2 and 3 introduce Biblical verses which point to Torah *she-beal peh*. The *posuk* (*Shmot* 34:27) quoted in question 3 according to the Gemara (*Gitten* 60b) refers to both *Torot*; G-d commands Moses to write "*hadevarim*" in the first clause, i.e., Torah *she-bektav*, while the "*devarim*" of the second clause refers to Torah *she-beal peh* as indicated by the phrase "*ki al pi*." In fact the Gemara (*ibid.*) derives the prohibition of writing Torah *she-beal peh* from this phrase. The remainder of lesson 28 introduces the great stress which *Yahadut* places on Torah *she-beal peh* with selections from *Gittin* (60b) and Yerushalmi, *Peah* (2:6) and *Megilla* (4:1). As mentioned in question 4, at the conclusion of these lessons (lesson 34) we shall return to this concept and attempt to place it in its proper perspective.

Lesson 29 considers the role played by Torah *she-beal peh* in arriving at the true meaning of Torah *bektav* either by supplying missing details or modifying the literal meaning of the text. Question 2 asks the student to identify different categories of *halachot*, using the laws of *tefillin* as a model, which illustrate the halachic methodology of Torah *she-beal peh*. Lesson 33 contains a fuller discussion of these categories. The halacha of *tefillin* was selected for two reasons. First, it is hoped that students will have a greater interest in and familiarity with these *halachot*. Second, it provides clear examples of the three major categories, viz., 1) *Halachot* transmitted directly from G-d to Moshe at Sinai which have not even the remotest basis in Torah *she-bektav*. These laws are called *halacha l'Moshe m'Sinai*. 2) *Halachot* transmitted at Sinai for which Biblical allusions may be found. 3) Rulings which the Rabbis inferred from the ordinary exegetical methods, the most famous of which are the 13 *middot* of Rabbi Yishmael. The classification and examples used here are borrowed from "*Mavo Hatalmud*" by Rabbi Zvi Hirsch Chayes which has been translated into English as "The Student's Guide Through The Talmud." The classic source is the Rambam's Introduction to his Commentary on the Mishna. The Rambam (*Tefillin* 1:3) lists ten *halachot* within the first category of *halacha l'Moshe m'Sinai*, e.g., the scriptural passages should be written in ink, on *klaf*, i.e., parchment on the side which faces the flesh. The boxes shall be square with the letter *shin* on the *shel rosh*, and the knot in the back of *shel rosh* should be in the shape of a *daled* so that together with the *yud* of the knot of *shel yad* one of G-d's names is formed.

The second category is comprised of laws which were transmitted orally at Sinai but for which the Rabbis have found an *asemachta* or hint in the written text, e.g., in *Sanhedrin* (4b) the Gemara deduces that four Scriptural passages are placed in the *Tefillin* from the word *totafot*, *tot* and *fot* each mean two in languages current in Biblical days. The final category are laws derived by the application of ordinary methods of interpretation (to be discussed in the lesson on Talmudic *drashot*), e.g., in *Menachot* (37a) it is derived that the tefillin *shel yad* are worn on the weak hand, and that *shel rosh* are not worn between the eyes as the text implies (derived from a *gezara shaveh*) but above the forehead where the hairline begins.

LESSON 30

THE MITZVA OF LIMUD TORAH

This lesson poses the critical question of why G-d saw fit to give part of this law in a written Torah and the remainder in oral form. Two answers are offered in the Student's Guide. First, an oral tradition insures the vital *talmid-rebbe* relationship so necessary to *Yahadut*. The Torah is more than an intellectual discipline; it is a comprehensive *derech hachayim* applicable to all aspects of life. As such it requires a rebbe whose behavior and character is to be emulated. Secondly, the difficulty inherent in the study of Torah *she-beal peh* has a function in regards to the mitzva of *limud Torah*.

At this point I would like to introduce a third answer to this question. The fact that Torah *she-beal peh* remained unwritten meant that it was inaccessible to other people. This of course should be contrasted with Torah *she-bektav* which was adopted by non-Jews who defiled it and claimed it as their own. The Midrash (*Yalkut Shimoni, Hosea* 8:12; Cf. Yerushalmi *Peah* 2:4 and *Tosafot, Gittin* 60b, s.v. *atmuhi* who quotes *Shmot Rabba* to the same effect) stress this factor.

"א״ר יהודה בר שלום בקש משה שתהא המשנה בכתב וצפה הקב״ה שעתידים עובדי אלילים לתרגם את התורה ולהיות קוראים בה יונית ואומרים אף הם ישראל אומר הקב״ה לאומות מה אתם אומרים שאתם

בני איני יודע אלא למי שמסטירין שלי בידו והוא בני ומהו המסטירין
זה משנה...".

"Rabbi Judah bar Shalom said: Moses wished that the Midrash should also be written down. G-d, however, foresaw that the gentiles would in time translate the Torah into Greek, and read it in Greek and say that they, too, are Israel. G-d says to the gentiles. Why do you say that you are My children? I consider only those as My children who possess My secrets. What are the secrets? The Mishna."

The first *parsha* of *Keriyat Shema* contains the answer to question 4 since it teaches us how to achieve *ahavat Hashem*. This is not a metaphysical mitzva meant only for philosophers. The Jew, even the simplest Jew, expresses his love of G-d by devoting his time and energy to the study of G-d's Torah.

LESSONS 31, 32

THE REDACTION OF TORAH SHE-BEAL PEH

These two lessons contain a brief review of the essentials of Jewish history in the Talmudic era. Primary emphasis is placed on the historic forces which led to the redaction or writing down of *Torah she-beal peh* in the Mishna and Gemara. If time permits the teacher should supplement the discussions contained in the Student's Guide with additional general historical background. I would recommend "Judaism" by Isidore Epstein, a short but excellent history in English, written from a traditional perspective by an acknowledged scholar.

It is my conviction that familiarity with the background and structure of the Talmud will make the "learning" experience more meaningful to the student. Questions 2 and 4 deal with the Mishna. The noun Mishna is derived from the verb *shanah*, 'to repeat'. It is of course an appropriate term for the Tannaim's method of study, since the oral law could be locked in memory only through constant repetition. Tannaim is derived from *tena*, the Aramaic equivalent of *shanah*. An extended discussion concerning the period when the Mishna was committed to writing is beyond the scope of this book. The Rambam insists in his introductions to both the Commentary on the Mishna and the Mishna Torah that

233

Rebbe actually wrote down the *Mishnayot*. A contrary opinion holds that Rebbe edited and arranged the *Mishnayot* systematically, with oral transmission continuing for several generations until the final redaction. The Talmud in *Yevamot* (64b) states:

"מתני מאן תקין רבי"

"Who compiled the Mishna? Rebbe." This of course is not conclusive proof to the Rambam's contention. Rabbi Z. H. Chayes has an excellent chapter discussing this problem in "*Mebo Ha-Talmud*" which has been translated into English as "The Student's Guide Through The Talmud" (New York, 1960 pp. 254-270).

Question 4 directs the student's attention to the six *sedarim* or orders of the Mishna. These *sedarim* can easily be recalled using the mnemonic *zeman nakot* which contains the first letter of each *seder*. The six *sedarim*, the number of *massechot* in each *seder*, and representative tractates within each *seder* follows.

    1) *Zeraim*, eleven tractates, including *Berakot, Peah, Kilayim, Terumot, Maasrot* etc.

    2) *Moed*, twelve tractates, including *Shabbat, Pesachim, Yoma, Succah, Beitza, Rosh Hashana, Megilla* etc.

    3) *Nashim*, seven tractates, including *Yevamot, Kettubot, Nedarim, Gittin, Kiddushin* etc.

    4) *Nezikin*, ten tractates, including *Baba Kamma, Baba Metzia, Baba Batra, Sanhedrin, Makkot, Avot,* etc.

    5) *Kodashim*, eleven tractates, including *Zevachim, Menachot, Chullin, Bechorot, Meilah* etc.

    6) *Tohorot*, twelve tractates, including *Kelim, Negaim, Mikvaot, Nidda* etc.

The term *shas* is derived from the first letters, *shin-*

samech, of *shisha sedarim*. *Rishonim* explain that the appela-
tion *Gaon* can properly be applied only to a scholar who has
mastered all of the tractates; the numerical value of the letters in *Gaon* equal sixty, the approximate number of *massechot*.

The lesson concludes with a question concerning *Geonim*,
Rishonim, and *Achronim*. The teacher will have to use his
own judgment in determining how detailed the discussions
devoted to this subject should be. At the very least the outstanding sages found in the standard editions of the Talmud
and the major commentaries should be placed in their proper
historical perspective. This information is readily available
and therefore no further discussion is warranted in this
volume.

LESSONS 33, 34

TALMUDIC METHODOLOGY: DRASHOT

It has been my experience that beginning students of Talmud encounter much difficulty in understanding and applying ordinary Talmudic methodology. Often this misunderstanding is sufficiently serious to prevent the student from developing an appreciation for "learning." These two lessons, therefore, focus on several of the more troublesome sore points, in an attempt to provide the student with a firm basis in methodological fundamentals. Lesson 33 begins with an analysis of the principle that the earlier the era, the more it is authoritative. Several logical and historical explanations are advanced in the Student's Guide to account for this situation.

Question 2 and the answer which follows discuss the existence of *machlokot* found in the Talmud. Much of the material in the Student's Guide has been developed from the Rambam's discussion in his Introduction to the Mishna. The teacher should stress, as the Rambam does, that *machlokot* do not appear in the first two categories of Torah *she-beal peh* i.e., those *halachot* transmitted to Moshe at Sinai for which support may be found in Torah *she-bektav*, and those known as *halacha l'Moshe Mi-Sinai* for which no scriptural support may be found. These of course are the two key categories. The great mass of *machlokot* are found in the third and fourth categories which are defined in the Student's Guide. The Rambam isolates a fifth category where *machlokot* are also found. This category embraces rules of behavior which are known as *takkanot* and *minhagim* and once accepted by the majority of Israel, have the force of law. Key selections from the Rambam's lengthy discussion follow.

„וזה עיקר יש לך לעמוד על סודו. והוא שהפירושים המקובלים מפי משה
אין מחלוקת בהם בשום פנים שהרי מאז ועד עתה לא מצאנו מחלוקת
נפלה בזמן מן הזמנים מימות משה ועד רב אשי בין החכמים כדי שיאמר
אחד המוציא עין חבירו יוציאו את עינו שנאמר 'עין בעין' ויאמר השני
אינו אלא כופר בלבד שחייב לתת, ולא מצאנו גם כן מחלוקת במה שאמר
הכתוב (ויקרא כ"ג) 'פרי עץ הדר' כדי שיאמר אחד שהוא אתרוג ויאמר
אחד שהוא חבושים או רמונים או זולתו ... לפיכך היו חלקי הדינים
המיוסדים בתורה על העיקרים האלה נחלקים לחמשה חלקים:
החלק הראשון פירושים מפי משה ויש להם רמז בכתוב ואפשר להוציאם
בדרך סברא וזה אין בו מחלוקת אבל כשיאמר האחד כך קבלתי אין
לדבר עליו:
החלק השני הם הדינים שנאמר בהן הלכה למשה מסיני ואין ראיות עליהם
כמו שזכרנו וזה כמו כן אין חולק עליו:
החלק השלישי הדינין שהוציאו על דרכי הסברא ונפלה בם מחלוקת כמו
שזכרנו ונפסק הדין בהן על פי הרוב וזה יקרה כשישתנה העיון ומפני
כך אומרים (יבמות דף ע"ו:) 'אם הלכה נקבל אם לדין יש תשובה'.
והחלק הרביעי הם הגזרות שתקנו הנביאים והחכמים בכל דור ודור כדי
לעשותם סייג לתורה, ועליהם צוה הקדוש ברוך הוא לעשותם והוא מה
שאמר (ויקרא י"ח) 'ושמרתם את משמרתי' ובאה בו הקבלה (יבמות כ"א)
'עשו משמרת למשמרתי'. והחכמים יקראו אותם גזרות, ולפעמים תפול
בהם מחלוקת לפי החכם שהוא אוסר כך מפני כך ולא יסכים עליו חכם אחר...
והחלק החמישי הם הדינים העשויים על דרך חקירה וההסכמה בדברים
הנוהגים בין בני אדם, שאין בם תוספת במצוה ולא גרעון, או בדברים שהם
תועלת לבני אדם בדברי תורה וקראו אותם תקנות ומנהגים".

Lesson 34 deals with the *middot* or exegetical rules of scriptural interpretation found in the Gemara. These *drashot* are probably the single most misunderstood and enigmatic item for the beginning student. In the Student's Guide, I have attempted to stress two important points. First, the *middot* themselves are part of *halacha l'Moshe mi-Sinai*. They were divinely fashioned and then transmitted to Moses. One of the commentators of the Rambam's "*Sefer Hamitzvot*" (*Kinat Sopherim*, end of *Shoresh Bet*) sums up the Rambam's principles of hermeneutics in the following manner.

„נמצינו למדים מתורתו של הרב הגדול הרמב״ם כמה כללים חמודים אמרתי לסדרן בקיצור: א) כלהו י״ג מדות ושאר לימודים שדרשו בהן חכמים הן ושימושיהן ותנאיהן מקובלות מסיני בכללות כדי שידונו בהן מעצמן לפרש ולבאר התורה שבכתב ומצותיה ודיניה ולא היה מחלוקת בהן בדורות ראשונים שהיו מתבררים ע״פ רובה של סנהדרין ובמשך הדורות וקלקול הזמנים ... נתעלמו ממנו ההלכות ... ב) באותן י״ג מדות ושאר לימודים היו דנין מעצמן חכמי הדורות זולתו בגזרת שוה לבדה עשו סייג וסדר הגון שלא לדון כל אדם מעצמו אא״כ קבלה מרבו ורבו מרבו ... ״

The second point is that Torah *she-bektav* was written by G-d with the same precision as found in the remainder of creation. Each superfluous word or letter, the usage of identical words in different passages (for *gezara shava*), the placing together of different subjects in one passage (for *hekesh*) etc., were all done purposefully.

In the Student's Guide, I have indicated that all *meforshim* agree that even *Chazal* could not fashion a *gezara shava* without the benefit of *masorah* stretching back to Sinai. However, there is a difference of opinion among *Rishonim* in regard to the necessity of *masorah* in the other *middot* of Rabbi Yishmael. Rashi (*Succah* 31a) holds that only a *kal vachomer* or logical inference could be made without the benefit of tradition. Most *Rishonim* including *Tosafot* (*Succah* 31a, s.v. *v'rav Yehuda*) and the Rambam ("*Sefer Hamitzvot*," *Shoresh Bet*) are of the opinion that *Chazal* could bring scriptural support to accepted teachings of Torah *she-*

beal peh by using the other exegetical devices even though they had no *mashorah* for the particular *drasha*.

The answer to question 3 which stresses the great role of Torah *she-beal peh* is developed extremely well by Rabbi Avigdor Miller in his valuable book "Rejoice O Youth!" (pp. 215-18). The lesson concludes with a discussion of *asmacheta*. Although many *meforshim* hold that often *asmachetot* were merely utilized as a pedagogical aid to memory, mention must be made of the famous opinion of the Ritva (*Rosh Hashana* 16a) that even *asmachtot* in support of Rabbinic laws were purposefully established by G-d in the written Torah. Although such laws are not binding *deoraitha*, G-d left the option open to the Rabbis to enact those rules they felt necessary and He provided the basis for such legislation in Torah *she-bektav*.

„שכל מה שיש לו אסמכתא מן הפסוק העיר הקב״ה שראוי לעשות כן אלא שלא קבעו חובה ומסרו לחכמים וזה דבר ברור ואמת ולא כדברי המפרשים האסמכתות שהוא כדרך סימן שנתנו חכמים ולא שכונת התורה לכך ח״ו ישתקע הדבר ולא יאמר שזו דעת מינות הוא אבל התורה העירה בכך ומסרה חיוב הדבר לקבעו חכמים אם ירצו כמו שכתוב 'ועשית על פי הדבר אשר יגידו לך' ולפיכך תמצא החכמים נותנין בכל מקום ראיה או זכר או אסמכתא לדבריהם מן התורה כלומר שאינם מחדשים דבר מלבם וכל תורה שבעל פה רמוזה בתורה שבכתב שהיא תמימה וח״ו שהיא חסירה כלום.״

LESSON 35

THE AGGADA

This lesson dealing with the Aggada follows naturally from the two preceding ones. In any discussion of Aggada it is essential that the student recognize that it is varied both in terms of its source and its pedagogical objective. The lesson begins with an analysis of the different types of Aggadic material. Primary emphasis must be placed on the first category, namely, those teachings which deal with the philosophic foundations of our faith. The student should recognize that Torah *min hashamayim* applies not only to halachic principles, but to philosophic principles as well. I have included in the Student's Guide a quotation in translation from Rabbi Z. H. Chayes' *"Mevo Ha-Talmud"* (p. 141, New York, 1960). The famous comment of Rabbeinu Chananel (*Succah* 45b) who stresses that *Chazal's* comments on such weighty matters must assuredly be part of the *masorah* from Moshe at Sinai bears repeating.

‏"...היה בידי הראשונים בקבלה כהלכה למשה מסיני. ואינם דבריהם שאלו הדברים וכיוצא בהן אי אפשר להאמר אלא בקבלה מן הנביאים ואלו הדברים שקיבלו מרבותיהם היו מגידים."‏

In the third class of *Aggadot*, i.e., those designed to impress upon Israel the importance of righteous behavior, *Chazal* often use classical exegetical devices so that their moral teachings might easily be remembered. The Rambam several times in the *"Moreh Nevuchim"* describes this practice and cautions against understanding such teachings literally (e.g., part 3:43). Similarly, the Rashba (commentary on *Berakot* 6a, published in *"Ein Yaakov"*) quoted in the Student's Guide stresses that certain *Aggadot* are clearly not to be understood literally, but are meant as allegories containing sublime secrets which *Chazal* meant to keep hidden from the ordinary student.

„הרשב"א כתב בספר מיוחד לפרש קצת הגדות וז"ל דע שיש לחכמים דברים נעלמים רמוזים במדרשים ובהגדות חתומים. ואם נגלו לעיני הסכלים כדברים בטלים, ליודעים חן ולמבינים הם ענינים שכליים. יש מן האגדות שלא נתנו להדרש אלא לבעלי הסודות, בהם רמזו לבעלי חכמה בנין ויסודות ..."

The lesson concludes with a question designed to acquaint the student with the classical *Midrashim*. Naturally, this is not the proper place for a detailed description of the *Midrashim*, but some elementary discussion is in order. The method of study known as *Midrash* should be distinguished from *Mishna*. In *Midrash* Torah *she-beal peh* was not studied independently of the written Torah, but instead it was taught as a commentary of Torah *she-bektav*. The earliest *Midrashim* were compiled in the second century by *Tannaim* who studied at the Yeshiva in Yavneh. These Tannaitic *Midrashim* generally contain more halachic and less aggadic material than the later *Midrashim*. The most famous are *Mechlita* on *Shmot* which was compiled by Rabbi Yishmael and his disciples, and the *Siphra* (also known as *Torat Cohanim*) on *Vayikra* and *Siphre* on *Bamidbar* and *Devarim* compiled by Rabbi Akiva's disciples, notably Rabbi Yehuda ben Ilai and Rabbi Shimon ben Yochai. The *Midrash Rabba* on all of *Chumosh* and part of *Nach* is a later collection, compiled at the end of the era of *Amoraim*.

LESSON 36

BECHIRAT CHAFSHIT: FREE WILL

In the fourth section of this book, I have attempted to develop a general theory of mitzvot and to describe *Chazal's* conception of the ultimate reward, both in this world and in *olam haba*, which depends upon observance of the mitzvot. Question 2 suggests that the principle of *bechirat chafshit* is the unifying element which makes possible both the system of divine law and reward and punishment. The Rambam (*Teshuva* 5:4) makes clear that man can be held accountable for his actions only if those actions result from a free, uncoerced choice.

The Rambam (*Teshuva* 5:1) discussed in the Student's Guide stresses that free-will is the great gift which distinguishes mankind from the remainder of G-d's creation. In the next halacha, Maimonides dismisses as the "opinion of the fools of the nations of the world" the doctrine of predestination so prominent in much of Islamic and Calvinist theology. "Let it not enter your mind that which the fools of the nations say and many of the unsophisticated Jews that G-d decrees at man's creation whether he is to be righteous or evil. This is not so but each human being can become as righteous as Moses or as wicked as Jeroboam; he can be wise or foolish, kind or cruel, miserly or generous or

any other traits . . . This is what Jeremiah said: 'Out of
the mouth of the Most High neither good nor evil proceed'
(Lamentations 3:38), i.e., it is not by G-d's decree that
man becomes good or evil." The *meforshim* explain that the
Rambam does not mean that it depends entirely upon the
individual whether he will become a *chacham*. Obviously not
all people are blessed with equal intellect. The meaning is
that it is up to the individual to develop his intellectual potential or allow it to be wasted.

„רשות לכל אדם נתונה אם רצה להטות עצמו לדרך טובה ולהיות צדיק
הרשות בידו ואם רצה להטות עצמו לדרך רעה ולהיות רשע הרשות בידו
הוא שכתוב בתורה 'הן האדם היה כאחד ממנו לדעת טוב ורע' כלומר הן
מין זה של אדם היה יחיד בעולם ואין מין שני דומה לו בזה העניין שיהא
הוא מעצמו בדעתו ובמחשבתו יודע הטוב והרע ועושה כל מה שהוא חפץ
ואין מי שיעכב בידו מלעשות הטוב או הרע וכיון שכן הוא פן ישלח ידו.
(ב) אל יעבור במחשבתך דבר זה שאומרים טפשי אוה״ע ורוב גולמי בני
ישראל שהקב״ה גוזר על האדם מתחלת ברייתו להיות צדיק או רשע אין
הדבר כן אלא כל אדם ראוי להיות צדיק כמשה רבינו או רשע כירבעם
או חכם או סכל או רחמן או אכזרי וכן שאר כל הדעות... הוא שירמיהו
אמר 'מפי עליון לא תצא הרעות והטוב' כלומר אין הבורא גוזר על האדם
להיות טוב ולא להיות רע ..."

Questions 1 and 4 analyze two aspects of the tension
between G-d's omnipotence and man's free-will. The student
should recognize that *bechirat chafshit* is as much a manifestation of G-d's will and control as any of the natural laws
which He built into the world. The far more serious philosophic problem is the apparent contradiction between divine
omniscience and human freedom. Most students will be satisfied with the Raavad's solution mentioned in the Student's
Guide that G-d's knowledge is not determinative. The Rambam's famous explanation (*Teshuva* 5:5) quoted below
should also be considered.

„שמא תאמר והלא הקב״ה יודע כל מה שיהיה וקודם שיהיה ידע שזה יהיה
צדיק או רשע, או לא ידע. אם ידע שהוא יהיה צדיק אי אפשר שלא יהיה
צדיק, ואם תאמר שידע שיהיה צדיק ואפשר שיהיה רשע הרי לא ידע הדבר
על בוריו. דע שתשובת שאלה זו ארוכה מארץ מדה ורחבה מני ים וכמה
עיקרים גדולים והררים רמים תלויים בה אבל צריך אתה לידע ולהבין
בדבר זה שאני אומר. כבר בארנו בפ׳ שני מהלכות יסודי התורה שהקב״ה
אינו יודע מדיעה שהיא חוץ ממנו כבני אדם שהם ודעתם שנים. אלא הוא
יתעלה שמו ודעתו אחד ואין דעתו של אדם יכולה להשיג דבר זה על
בוריו וכשם שאין כח באדם להשיג ולמצוא אמתת הבורא שנאמר ׳כי לא
יראני האדם וחי׳ כך אין כח באדם להשיג ולמצוא דעתו של בורא ...
וכיון שכן הוא אין בנו כח לידע היאך ידע הקב״ה כל הברואים והמעשים
אבל נדע בלא ספק שמעשה האדם ביד האדם ואין הקב״ה מושכו ולא גוזר
עליו לעשות כך. ולא מפני קבלת הדת בלבד נודע דבר זה אלא בראיות
ברורות מדברי החכמה. ומפני זה נאמר בנבואה שדנין את האדם על מעשיו
כפי מעשיו אם טוב רע ואם רע וזה הוא העיקר שכל דברי הנבואה תלויין בו״.

"You may ask, G-d knows all that will happen. Before someone becomes a good or a bad man, G-d either knows that this
will happen or He does not know it. If He knows that the
person will be good is it impossible for that person to be
bad? If you answer that while G-d knows that he will be
good it is still possible for him to be bad, then G-d has no
clear foreknowledge. Know that the solution to this problem
is larger than the earth and wider than the sea, many essential principles of faith and mountains of thought depend
upon it. But it is necessary for you to grasp thoroughly that
which I am about to say. We have already explained in the
second chapter of *hilchot yesodei Hatorah* that G-d does not
know with a knowledge that is apart from Him, like human
beings whose self and knowledge are distinct one from the
other. G-d's knowledge and His Self are one and the same
though no human being is capable of clearly comprehending
this matter. Just as it is beyond human capacity to comprehend or discover G-d's true nature, as it says: 'For man shall
not see me and live' (*Shmot* 33:20), so it is beyond human

capacity to comprehend or discover G-d's knowledge . . . It follows that we are incapable of comprehending how G-d knows all creatures and all deeds. But this we do know beyond any doubt, that man's deeds are in his own hands, G-d neither compelling him nor determining that he should behave in a certain way. It is not alone through religious tradition that we know this to be so but by means of clear philosophical truths. Because of this, prophecy teaches that man is judged on his deeds according to those deeds, whether good or evil. All the words of prophecy depend on this principle."

The explanation in the Student's Guide of the Rambam's distinction between G-d's knowledge and human knowledge is based on the comment of the *Tosafot Yom Tov* to the Mishna in *Avot* (3:15).

OLAM HABA AND YEMOT HAMASHIACH

Bechirat Chafshit leads to the principle of *schar v'onesh,* which states that each human being is ultimately responsible for his actions. However, before we can analyze this subject, it is necessary to develop at least an elementary understanding of the concepts of *olam haba, yemot hamashiach,* and *techiyat hamatim.* Only then can 'reward and punishment' be understood in a meaningful manner. It has been my experience that few fundamental areas of Jewish thought are the subject of as much ignorance and misconception among students as these. The teacher, therefore, should take nothing for granted in his exposition. Conversely, few topics interest and excite students as much as these do.

Lesson 37 begins with Maimonides' (*Teshuva* 8:6) explanation for the lack of precise detail in *Tanach* describing *olam haba.* Since the first stage of *olam haba* involves a purely spiritual state—and we know only this world—it is not possible to appreciate the goodness which awaits in the world to come. The Rambam (*Teshuva* 8:7 quoted below, and Commentary to the Mishna, *Sanhedrin* 10:1) continues that the prophets confined their prophecy to the Messianic era which will occur in this world, but were silent concerning *olam haba,* lest their description of *olam haba* appear trifling by com-

parison to the vivid and readily comprehensible images of
yemot hamashiach.

‏»כבר הודיעונו החכמים הראשונים שטובת העולם הבא אין כח באדם
להשיגה על בוריה ואין יודע גדלה ויפיה ועצמה אלא הקב״ה לבדו. ושכל
הטובות שמתנבאים בהם הנביאים לישראל אינן אלא לדברים שבגוף שנהנין
בהן ישראל לימות המשיח בזמן שתשוב הממשלה לישראל אבל טובת חיי
העולם הבא אין לה ערך ודמיון ולא דמוה הנביאים כדי שלא יפחתו אותה
בדמיון . . . «

This analysis may be made more meaningful as students
in the classroom attempt to answer the problem posed in
question 2. The teacher should point out that as man matures
things which were once of vital importance, pale into significance. Just as the diamond means nothing to the infant and
very much to the adult, so too the pleasures of *olam haba*
become meaningful only after we pass from this world into
the next. We should at this point indicate that Nachmanides
stresses in the *"Shaar Ha-Gemul"* that *Chazal's* discussions
in the Talmud and particularly the *Midrash of Gan Eden*
refer to this first stage of *olam haba.* The lesson concludes
with several references from *Tanach* to *olam haba.* The Ramban's argument that it is logically inconceivable for man's
soul which comes from G-d to be subject to death is quoted
in translation in the Student's Guide and is reproduced
below.

‏»נשמת האד נר ה׳ אשר נופחה באפינו מפי עליון ונשמת שדי כמו שנאמר
‏'ויפח באפיו נשמת חיים׳ והנה היא בעניינה ולא תמות . . . אבל קיומה
ראויה והיא עומדת לעד.«

Lesson 38 of the Student's Guide contains a fairly complete analysis of *Chazal's* conception of the Messianic era.
The teacher should supplement this material with the Rambam's concluding passage of the *"Mishna Torah"* (*Melachim*
12:5) which describes the ultimate perfection this world can
know.

„ובאותו הזמן לא יהיה שם לא רעב ולא מלחמה ולא קנאה ותחרות שהטובה
תהיה משופעת הרבה וכל המעדנים מצויין כעפר ולא יהיה עסק כל העולם
אלא לדעת את ה׳ בלבד ולפיכך יהיו ישראל חכמים גדולים ויודעים דברים
הסתומים וישיגו דעת בוראם כפי כח האדם״.

The final lesson devoted to Judaism's eschatological views
examines the doctrine of *techiyat hamatim*. Maimonides in
both the Commentary to the Mishna and the "*Mishna Torah*"
makes only passing reference to physical resurrection which
prompted some of his contemporaries to assume that in fact
he denied this doctrine. In response to such speculation, the
Rambam wrote "*Maamar Techiyat Hamatim*", an essay devoted entirely to this topic. In defense of his taciturnity in
his philosophical and halachic works, the Rambam explains
that there is very little one can say concerning *techiyat
hamatim* since it cannot be proven by philosophic speculation and is necessarily shrouded in mystery and secrecy.
However, the Ramabam very clearly states the fundamental
importance of this doctrine in Judaism's scheme of things in
the following statement from the "*Maamar Techiyat Hamatim.*" "I say that the meaning of *techiyat hamatim*—a doctrine renowned and accepted among our people and acknowledged by every one of our group and mentioned frequently
in the prayers, narratives and supplications which were composed by the prophets and the great sages and which fill the
pages of the Talmud and the *Midrash*—is that the soul will
return to the body after it has been separated from it. Among
our nation there is no difference of opinion on this matter,
no dissenting voice. It is not permitted to place any reliance
on any member of our religion who does not believe in this."

Nevertheless, Maimonides believes that the ultimate state
of man is spiritual. After a long period on earth, the revived
body dies again and the soul returns to an eternal *olam haba*.
This contention is firmly rejected by Nachmanides in the
"*Shaar Ha-Gemul*" who says (in the following passage which

concludes that essay) that the Rambam alone of all Jewish
philosophers held such a view. All other Jewish thinkers
definitely hold that the reunited body and soul exist in an
eternal world, "*she-kulo aruch*."

„והכל מודים בתחיית המתים ובקיום הזמן ההוא ... זולת דעת הרב רבי
משה [בן מימון] ז"ל שנותנת קצבה לזמן התחיה ומחזיר הכל לעולם הנשמות
ואנחנו מקיימים אנשי התחיה לעדי עד מימות תחיית המתים לעוה"ב שהוא
עולם שכולו ארוך".

The discussion in answer to question 1 gives several Biblical references in support of the *masorah* of *techiyat hamatim*.
Many other such examples may be found in the Gemara
(particularly *Sanhedrin* 91a and b) among which is the
famous statement of Rabbi Meir:

„תניא אמר רבי מאיר מניין לתחיית המתים מן התורה שנאמר 'אז ישיר
משה ובני ישראל את השירה הזאת לה' " 'שר' לא נאמר אלא 'ישיר' מכאן
לתחיית המתים מן התורה".

Question 3 directs the student's attention to the text of
hakol yoducha which is part of the first of the *birchot keriyat Shema* in the Shabbat *Shachrit* service. The order of the
phrases in the quoted selection is significant. There is none
to be compared with G-d in each of the four stages through
which man passes, *olam hazeh, olam haba, yemot hamashiach*
and *techiyat hamatim*. The lesson concludes with the relevant
selection from *Yigdal*. The quoted selection follows in translation. "At time's end He will send our Messiah to save all
who wait for His final help. G-d, in his great mercy, will
revive the dead. Blessed be His glorious name forever."

LESSON 40

SCHAR V'ONESH

The eleventh principle of faith formulated by Maimonides is the belief in individual reward and punishment.

„היסוד אחד עשר כי הוא הש״י נותן שכר למי שעושה מצות התורה ויעניש
למי שעובר על אזהורותיה וכי השכר הגדול העולם הבא והעונש החזק
הכרת ... והמקרה המורה על היסוד הזה מה שנאמר (שמות לב: לב) 'ועתה
אם תשא חטאתם — ואם אין מחני נא' והשיב לו הש״י 'מי אשר חטא
לי אמחנו מספרי' ראיה שיודע העובר והחוטא לתת שכר לזה ועונש לזה".

"The eleventh principle of faith that He, the exalted one, rewards the one who obeys the commands of the Torah, and punishes the one who transgresses its prohibitions. The greatest reward is *olam haba*, and the strongest punishment is *karet*, cutting off . . . The verse which teaches this principle is: 'Now if You will forgive their sin—; but if not, blot me out of your book' (*Shmot* 32:32). And G-d replied to him: 'Whoever has sinned against Me, him will I blot from My book' (*Shmot* 32:33). This is proof of what the obedient and the rebellious each receive. G-d rewards the one and punishes the other."

It is apparent from this selection that the Rambam (the Ramban concurs in *Shaar Ha-Gemul*) considers that true reward is granted in the eternal *olam haba* rather than in the temporal *olam hazeh*. Nevertheless, (as the discussion in

answer to question 3 indicates) the Rambam in *Teshuva*
(9:1), quoted below, does not deny that observance of the
mitzvot brings with it substantial benefits in this world.
However, such benefits as long life, wealth and peace are not
in themselves the ultimate *schar*. Instead they make it possible for the individual to perform still more mitzvot and
thereby accumulate additional reward which will ultimately
be enjoyed in *olam haba*.

„מאחר שנודע שמתן שכרן של מצות והטובה שנזכה לה אם שמרנו דרך ה'
הכתוב בתורה היא חיי העולם הבא שנאמר 'למען ייטב לך והארכת ימים',
והנקמה שנוקמים מן הרשעים שעזבו ארחות הצדק הכתובות בתורה היא
הכרת שנאמר 'הכרת תכרת הנפש ההיא עונה בה', מהו זה שכתוב בכל
התורה כולה אם תשמעו יגיע לכם כך ואם לא תשמעו יקרה אתכם כך
וכל אותן הדברים בעולם הזה, כגון שובע ורעב ומלחמה ושלום ומלכות
ושפלות וישיבת הארץ וגלות והצלחת מעשה והספדו ושאר כל דברי הברית.
כל אותן הדברים אמת היו ויהיו ובזמן שאנו עושים כל מצות התורה יגיעו
אלינו טובות העולם הזה כולן, ובזמן שאנו עוברים עליהן תקראנה אותנו
הרעות הכתובות. ואף על פי כן אין אותן הטובות הם סוף מתן שכרן של
מצות ולא אותן הרעות הם סוף הנקמה שנוקמין מעובר על כל המצות.
אלא כך הוא הכרע כל הדברים. הקב"ה נתן לנו תורה זו עץ חיים היא
וכל העושה כל הכתוב בה ויודעו דעה גמורה נכונה זוכה בה לחיי העולם
הבא. ולפי גודל מעשיו ורוב חכמתו הוא זוכה. והבטיחנו בתורה שאם נעשה
אותה בשמחה ובטובת נפש ונהגה בחכמתה תמיד שיסיר ממנו כל הדברים
המונעים אותנו מלעשותה כגון חולי ומלחמה ורעב וכיוצא בהן. וישפיע
לנו כל הטובות המחזיקות את ידינו לעשות התורה כגון שובע ושלום ורבוי
כסף וזהב, כדי שלא נעסוק כל ימינו בדברים שהגוף צריך להן אלא נשב
פנויים ללמוד בחכמה ולעשות המצוה כדי שנזכה לחיי העולם הבא".

Question 2 involves the first Mishna of *Peah*. The translation of the quoted selection follows: "These are the things
of which a man enjoys the fruits in this world, while the
principal remains for him in *olam haba*: honoring one's
parents, the practice of kindness, the making of peace between
fellow men; but the study of Torah exceeds them all." The

Rambam in his commentary to this Mishna explains that *gemilat chasadim* involves two types of virtuous behavior: aiding one's fellow economically, e.g., charity, redeeming prisoners (which certainly applies to contemporary Russian Jewry), honest and faithful business dealings, and physically, e.g., visiting the sick and mourners, honoring the deceased etc. The Rambam then distinguishes between *gemilat chasadim* and the other mitzvot mentioned in question 2. The former involve not only man and G-d, but man and his fellow man; they are mitzvot *bein adam l'chaveiro* as well as mitzvot *bein adam la'makom*. Mitzvot such as *tefillin, Shabbat, matzo*, etc., are solely *bein adam la'makom*. It is appropriate that precepts within the category of *gemilat chasadim* provide fruits in this world, corresponding to the righteous conduct extended to fellow men, as well as *schar* in *olam haba* which results from observing any of G-d's commands. However, according to Maimonides, mitzvot which are solely *bein adam la'makom* are rewarded primarily in *olam haba*.

LESSON 41

TZADIK V'RA LO

Lesson 41 deals with the most enigmatic problem which confronts any religion—the question of the suffering of the righteous and the happiness of the wicked. This very problem prompted the opinion of Rabbi Yaakov mentioned in the last lesson, namely, reward for righteous behavior is granted solely in *olam haba*. He asks (*Kiddushin* 39b), "What if a father sent his son to bring some young birds?" The boy did so, fulfilling the command of *kibud av*, and, in addition, he sent away the mother before taking the young thereby fulfilling the mitzva of *shiluach hakan*. On the way home, the boy fell and died. Here the boy has fulfilled two mitzvot for which the Torah promises long life—what has become of the Torah's promise? Rabbi Yaakov replies, "the promise will be fulfilled in the world to come."

However, most of *Chazal* hold that the principle of *schar v'onesh* applies to this world, as well as the next. How can we explain *tzadik v'ra lo* . . . according to them? In the Student's Guide, I have attempted to present the approach of the *ben Torah*. First, outward appearances are often deceiving. The standard measure of success, wealth, power, prestige etc., do not guarantee happiness. Furthermore, dedication to G-d's will, in and of itself, constitutes a significant reward, since it provides meaning in the midst of a world of mystery to one's existence. The Gemara (*Berakot* 5a) supplies an important concept to fill in Judaism's response to this enigma.

„אמר רבא אם רואה אדם שיסורין באין עליו יפשפש במעשיו שנאמר 'נחפשה דרכינו ונחקורה ונשובה עד ה' פשפש ולא מצא יתלה בבטול תורה שנאמר 'אשרי הגבר אשר תיסרנו יה ומתורתך תלמדנו' ואם תלה ולא מצא בידוע שיסורין של אהבה הם שנאמר 'כי את אשר יאהב ה' יוכיח".

"Rava says: If a man see that suffering comes upon him, let him examine his conduct, for it says, 'Let us search and examine our ways, and return unto the Lord' (Lamentations 3:40). If he examines and finds nothing, he should attribute [the suffering] to his neglect of the study of Torah, for it says, 'Happy is the man whom G-d chastizes and teaches from His Torah' (Psalm 94:12). If he did attribute it thus and still did not [find it to be the cause], he can be certain that these are sufferings of love, for it says, 'He whom G-d loves, He corrects' (Proverbs 3:12)." Rashi explains that *yissurim shel ahava* is suffering brought by G-d upon an individual in this world not as atonement for sin, but as a means of increasing that person's *schar* in *olam haba*. In *Baba Metzia* (85a) in connection with the suffering of both Rav Eleazar, the son of Rav Shimon bar Yochai, and Rebbe, the Talmud expands upon the concept of *yissurin shel ahava*. Beside the ultimate reward in *olam haba*, such suffering also has beneficial consequences for the community at large. In the words of the "*Chidushei Geonim*" quoted in "*Ein Yaakov*" (*ibid.*):

„והאל יתברך שהכל גלוי לפניו ראה וידע שלא היה בהם שמץ פיסול עון והביא עליהם היסורין מאהבה להרבות שכרם לתועלת הדור ותועלתם בעולם הבא".

LESSONS 42, 43

THE PURPOSE OF THE MITZVOT

The remainder of this book deals with the mitzvot—the first three lessons set forth a general conceptual framework of mitzvot, followed by an analysis of specific mitzvot. Lesson 42 begins with the famous midrashic statement of Rav:

"רב אמר לא נתנו המצות אלא לצרף בהן את הבריות. וכי מה איכפת ליה להקב"ה למי ששוחט מן הצואר או מי ששוחט מן העורף".

As explained by the Ramban (*Devarim* 22:6; Cf. *"Moreh Nevuchim"* 3:26), the Midrash teaches us that the purpose of the mitzvot is not for G-d—"what difference does it make to G-d whether an animal is killed by cutting the neck in front or in the back?"—but as a means of purifying Israel so that we may be *goy kadosh*. A particular mitzva brings man closer to G-d by either inculcating a positive moral or ethical trait, or by protecting man from improper thought and evil conduct.

Question 2 points out that the two integral aspects of *kadosh* apply to the halachic concept of *hekdesh*. An object which is donated to the Temple is set apart from *chol*, the mundane, and becomes *kadosh*. As such it is dedicated and sanctified for use only in the *Bet Hamikdash*. The people of Israel, individually and collectively, likewise must be set apart

255

from the rest of mankind, if we are to be the *am kadosh* and dedicate ourselves to G-d's service.

The remainder of this lesson stresses a crucial difference in attitude between that of Judaism and that of Christianity. This distinction is necessary in order to arrive at a meaningful appreciation of the role of mitzvot. Unlike Christianity, Judaism does not view negatively the physical side of man's life. The *posuk* quoted in the Student's Guide (*Bereshit* 2:7) indicates the delicate balance Judaism strikes between the physical and spiritual aspects of man. In fact, as Rashi comments, the word *vayizer* appears with two *yudin* to indicate that each individual's initial creation relates to both *olam hazeh* and *olam haba*. Judaism of course absolutely forbids celibacy, and in general, frowns upon asceticism. The halacha is structured to reinforce this delicate balance; man should strive for a middle ground between a life of the flesh and one of the spirit. Question 4 points out that the *Nazir* is required to offer several *korbonot*, including a *chatos*, a sin offering, at the conclusion of his *nazirut*. Among the explanations advanced by *Chazal* to explain the need for a *korbon chatos* is that of Rabbi Eleazar Hakappor: "His sin consists in that he has afflicted himself by abstaining from the enjoyment of wine" (*Nazir* 19a; *Taanit* 11a). He has sinned against himself by denying himself an enjoyment permitted by the Torah.

Physical conduct must also be *avodat Hashem*. The mitzvot provide the means to transform mundane physical acts into service of the Lord. The remainder of this lesson illustrates this process by focusing upon eating. A simple meal without any obvious religious connotation becomes *avodat Hashem* if the proper *bracha rishona* and *bracha achrona* are recited. Furthermore, the act of eating is often a positive mitzva, e.g. *shalosh seudot*, matzo on Passover, s*euda hamafseket* on Erev Yom Kippur etc.

Lesson 43 attempts to combat an extremely serious misconception which is shared by many students, and often by their parents as well. It is fashionable in some circles to view the mitzvot as an all-encompassing, rigorous system which stifles individual freedom. It is our duty to impress upon the students the *mitzvot's* liberating function. Perhaps the most oppressive tyranny which can enslave man is self-tyranny— the individual's submission to his uncontrolled physical desires. We need only look about us to see a major segment of American youth who in their pathetic rebellion against authority, have subjected themselves to this most cruel form of slavery. The mitzvot, which force man to think before he acts, perform the extremely valuable function of making reason rather than *yetzer* the decisive factor in man's conduct. Once again, I have selected eating, probably the most basic of man's instincts, to illustrate this process. Question 2 points out that various hygenic explanations for particular food prohibitions, although often scientifically accurate, are irrelevant to the far more important purpose of training man in the control of a basic instinctive drive.

The teacher depending upon the maturity of his class, might at this point show that halacha performs this same function in regulating the sexual relationship of husband and wife. The law of *nidda*, besides it obvious role in promoting a healthy sexual environment for husband and wife, also insures the individual's control over a normal human drive. The separation of at least twelve days' duration during the wife's menstrual period insures that the couple's physical relationship does not become stale. Each month the honeymoon is recreated. Equally important, during menstruation desire is replaced by self-discipline, instinct is controlled by reason.

LESSON 44

TAAMEI HAMITZVOT

This lesson deals at some length with *taamei hamitzvot*, the purpose underlying a particular precept. The lesson begins with an analysis of the reason for the great multitude of mitzvot. The Mishna (*Makkot* 23b) which is quoted in the Student's Guide explains that the purpose for the profusion of mitzvot found in the Torah is that the Jew should merit divine reward for his conduct—even such conduct as would be followed in the absence of a specific command. The comment of Rashi to this Mishna is significant.

‫"לזכות את ישראל — כדי שיהיו מקבלין שכר במה שמונעין עצמן מן‬
‫העבירות לפיכך הרבה להן שלא היה צורך לצוות כמה מצות וכמה אזהרות‬
‫על שקצים ונבלות שאין לך אדם שאינו קץ בהן אלא כדי שיקבלו שכר‬
‫על שפורשין מהן".‬

The discussion in response to question 2 makes clear that there is reason and purpose for each of the 613 mitzvot, *chukkim* as well as *mishpatim*. We would of course expect such an approach from Maimonides (whose view is quoted in the Student's Guide), the great rationalist, but in fact Jewish philosophers are in unanimous agreement concerning this principle. The statement of the Ramban (*Vayikra* 19:19) is representative.

258

»וכן חוקי הקב״ה הם הסודות אשר לו בתורה שאין העם במחשבתם נהגים
בהם כמשפטים אבל כלם בטעם נכון ותועלת שלימה.«

Question 4 asks why the reasons underlying particular mitzvot are often not revealed in the Torah. The Talmud (*Sanhedrin* 21b) addresses itself to the question.

»אמר רב יצחק מפני מה לא נתגלו טעמי התורה שהרי שתי מקראות נתגלו
טעמן נכשל בהן גדול העולם כתיב ׳לא ירבה לו נשים׳אמר שלמה אני
ארבה ולא אסור וכתיב ׳ויהי לעת זקנת שלמה נשיו הטו את לבבו׳ וכתיב
׳לא ירבה לו סוסים׳ ואמר שלמה אני ארבה ולא אשיב׳ וכתיב ׳ותצא
מרכבה ממצרים בשש.«

"Rabbi Yitzchak said: Why were the reasons of some Biblical laws not revealed? Because in two verses reasons were revealed, and they caused the greatest in the world [Solomon] to stumble. It is written, 'He shall not multiply wives to himself' [*Devarim* 17:17] whereon Solomon said, 'I will multiply wives and not let my heart be perverted.' Nevertheless, we are taught, 'When Solomon was old, his wives turned away his heart' [1 *Melachim* 11:4]. Again it is written, 'He shall not multiply to himself horses' [in order not to cause the people to return to Egypt, the leading horse market. *Devarim* 17:17] concerning which Solomon said, 'I will multiply them, but will not cause [Israel] to return [to Egypt].' Yet it is written, 'And a chariot came up and went out of Egypt for six [hundred shekels of silver]' [1 *Melachim* 10:29, i.e., the Israelites traveled to Egypt for the purpose of trade.]" G-D's purpose in not revealing all *taamei hamitzvot* is apparent from this passage. As long as the reason remains unknown, man is protected from his own arrogance; he is not tempted to place his own rationality above *taamei hamitzvot*.

LESSONS 45, 46, 47

SYMBOLIC MITZVOT

In these three lessons we turn from a consideration of
the general purposes underlying mitzvot to an analysis of
the specific content of several symbolic mitzvot. It is important that students recognize that there is nothing unique
in Judaism's use of symbols. All cultures employ symbols to
represent ideas. Abstractions are made real through the use
of symbols, inherently meaningless, but definitely meaningful once an association between the symbol and the concept
it represents is made.

The first two questions of lesson 45 suggest an important
difference between the symbols of Judaism in the form of
symbolic mitzvot, and those common to all mankind. Since
the mitzvot are G-d's creation, it is not surprising that they
often contain utilitarian values. In other words, mitzvot are
multi-faceted; their obvious meaning does not begin to describe the total complex. Question 1 asks the student to analyze the symbolic meaning of three mitzvot. By refraining
on *Shabbat* from *melacha*, creative work, the Jew impresses
upon himself that he owes his creative ability to G-d, the
Supreme Creator. Similarly, the precept of *shmita* impresses
upon the Jew that G-d is the master of nature. Despite a
farmer's toil and struggle caring for his crops, his ultimate

success depends upon G-d's blessing. Finally, *brit milah* symbolizes physically the convenant between Israel and G-d. Question 2 focuses on the utilitarian aspects of these mitzvot. The *menucha* which results from refraining from *melacha* enables the Jew to rejuvenate himself physically and emotionally. The cares and tensions which are part of life are replaced, at least for a day, with spiritual contentment. We cannot overestimate the role of *Shabbat* in promoting physical and emotional well-being. The mitzva of *shmita* provides a similar utilitarian service. Modern science has only recently discovered that leaving land fallow enables nature to rejuvenate the soil for continued productivity. Similarly, *brit milah* provides an important benefit wholly apart from its symbolic meaning. Scientific studies indicate that circumcision protects both husband and wife from various diseases, including cancer. For centuries, "enlightened" men mocked Judaism for this "barbaric" practice. Today it is universally practiced. Certainly such side benefits are not crucial in our observance of these mitzvot. We observe the law because it is G-d's will. Nevertheless, they are relevant as an aid in developing in our students a greater appreciation for the mitzvot. Furthermore, these utilitarian benefits have only recently been recognized by mankind. What further benefits await future discovery in these and other mitzvot is beyond human contemplation.

In the remainder of this lesson, two mitzvot, *gid hanasheh* and *chometz*, are examined in order to discover their symbolic content. Much of the material is based upon an excellent essay by Dr. Dayan Grunfeld which appeared in *Traditional* (vol. 4, no 2). The answer to question 3 is clear. By refraining from eating *gid hanasheh*, we symbolically affirm our belief in Israel's ultimate victory despite temporary setbacks, pain and suffering.

Lesson 46 is devoted to an analysis of the purpose of three

related mitzvot—*tefillin*, *mezuzah* and *tzitzit*. By wearing
tefillin on the left arm directly adjacent to the heart, and on
the head, we symbolically affirm that our actions, emotions
and intellect are placed into G-d's service. Question 2 poses
the problem of why *tefillin* are not worn on *Shabbat* and
Yom Tov. *Chazal* explain that since *Shabbat* and *Yom Tov*,
as well as *tefillin*, serve as a sign of the covenant between
G-d and Israel, the wearing of *tefillin* on these days is superfluous. However, there is a difference of opinion among *pos-
kim* concerning *tefillin* on *Chol Hamoed* (*Orach Hayim* 31:2).
Consequently, two *minhagim* have developed. Most Ashkenazim put on *tefillin* on *Chol Hamoed*, while Sephardim ordinarily do not.

Question 3 asks for the significance of placing a *mezuza*
in each room of the house. As indicated in the Student's
Guide (*Menachot* 23b), *mezuza*, along with *tefillin* and
tzitzit, constantly reminds the Jew of who he is and how he
must act. This reminder obviously should not be limited to
a particular room; it is fitting and proper that it should be
placed before us at all times. The yarmulka is a practice
which serves a similar function. It is beyond the scope of
this volume to engage in a discussion of the halachic implications of the head-covering requirement. Nevertheless, the
famous statement in *Kiddushin* (31a) is relevant.

‫"רב הונא לא מסגי ארבע אמות בגילוי הראש אמר שכינה למעלה מראשי".‬

"Rav Huna would not walk four cubits with his head un-
covered. He said the Shechina is above my head." The
covered head indicates both respect before G-d, and serves
as an important influence on the individual's behavior. It
has, today, assumed enormous significance as a vivid symbol
of allegiance to our faith, and as a concrete manifestation of
Jewish self-pride.

Question 4 deals with the role of *tzitzit*. The numerical

value of the letters which comprise the word *tzitzit* equals
600 which together with the eight fringes and five knots on
each corner of the garment totals 613. Since the Torah tells
us that *tzitzit* serve as a reminder of *taryag* mitzvot, the
number 613 is most appropriate.

All of lesson 47 is devoted to the mitzva of shatnes in an
attempt to correct some popular misconceptions and to indicate the deep religious symbolism of this often neglected
mitzva *deoraitha*. The fact that a label "100% pure wool"
appears is no guarantee that a garment is free of shatnes.
Button-holes, lining and collar may still be sewn with linen.
Another common error which should be corrected is that this
precept applies only to men's clothing. Since it is a mitzva
lo taaseh, a negative prohibition, it applies equally to men
and women.

In the Student's Guide, the Ramban's interpretation is
introduced. The three *kilayim mitzvot* in their totality are
a symbolic reminder of man's technological limits, and an
implicit acknowledgement of G-d's creation. The following
selection from Nachmanides' commentary (*Vayikra* 19:19)
develops this theme in its stress upon man's arrogance in
attempting to improve upon creation.

„והטעם בכלאים כי השם ברא המינים בעולם בכל בעלי הנפשות בצמחים
ובבעלי נפש התנועה ונתן בהם כח התולדה שיתקיימו המינים בהם לעד ...
והמרכיב שני מינים משנה ומכחיש במעשה בראשית כאלו יחשוב שלא
השלים הקב״ה בעולמו כל הצורך ויחפוץ הוא לעזור בבריאתו של עולם
להוסיף בו בריות."

The Ramban (*ibid.*) also discusses the problem posed in
question 3. G-d structured creation so that each species re-
produces itself *l'mineihu* and nature therefore rejects any
attempt at breeding unrelated species. So, for example, the
mating of a cat with a dog will not be successful. The mating of related species which does produce offspring supports

this principle. Although a horse and donkey can be bred to produce a mule, this offspring is sterile.

The Mishna (*Kilayim* 9:8) explains the derivation of the word shatnes called for by question 4. It is an abbreviation of three Hebrew words, *shua*, which means pressed, *tavuy*, woven, and *nuz*, twisted. The prohibition, therefore, extends to any material which contains wool and linen which have been woven, braided or pressed (e.g., felt) together.

LESSON 48

THE STATUS OF WOMEN IN JUDAISM

The tumult and massive publicity engendered by the attempt of women to redefine their place in society has definite implications for Judaism, and particularly for the teacher of Jewish youth. Superficially, at least, traditional Judaism appears vulnerable to a charge that it relegates women to a position of inferiority. This accusation results from two circumstances. First, the religious duties incumbent upon women is less extensive than those upon men, and secondly, the requirement of the *mechitza* in the synagogue. The thrust of the discussion in the Student's Guide is that these circumstances do not imply any inferiority in the status of women. Rather, they indicate Judaism's sensitivity to the unique capability of women.

It is stressed in the Student's Guide that the majority of mitzvot—all the negative commandments and the positive commandments which do not depend upon a specific time— apply equally to *nashim*. Furthermore, the exemption from fulfilling mitzvot *asheh she-hazeman gerama* is based upon the woman's natural superiority in raising and caring for children—a task so important that it prevails over certain mitzvot. Nevertheless, as question 2 points out, women who fulfill these mitzvot receive *schar* for their observance (*Kid-*

dushin 31a) and recite the standard *birkat hamitzva* (*ibid.,*
Tosafot, s.v. *delo*). Women customarily observe such mitzvot *aseh she-hazeman gerama* as Shofar, Succah, Lulav and
Esrog, etc. Question 3 asks for exceptions to the general
rule, time-dependent mitzvot which are binding upon *nashim.*
The two most important examples are matza on Pesach and
kiddush on *Shabbat* and *Yom Tov* (See Ramban, *Avodat
Cochavim* 12:3). The Talmud (*Pesachim* 43b) explains that
the positive commandment of matza applies to all those involved in the negative prohibition of chometz. Similarly, in
Berakot (20b) the Talmud explains that *zachor* appears once
in *asseret hadibrot* and *shamor* in the other version to teach
us that all who are involved in *shemirat Shabbat* must also
fulfill *zechirat Shabbat* i.e., *kiddush hayom.*

The remainder of the lesson is devoted to an analysis of
the *mechitza* requirement. An extremely valuable volume
entitled "The Sanctity of the Synagogue" edited by Baruch
Litvin, contains many selections in English translation of
the statements of *gedolei yisroel,* past and present, concerning this topic. In the Student's Guide I have attempted to
accomplish two things. The student should recognize both
the halachic and historical significance of the *mechitza,* and
also its practical role of promoting the mood and atmosphere
necessary for communication with the Almighty.

The construction of a woman's balcony in the Temple
(*Succah* 51b) should not be understood to imply that before
this innovation mingling of the sexes was permitted. The
Gemara states (*ibid.*): "The women stood outside the court-
yard, and the men stood inside." Because of the fear that
even with such an arrangement there would still be improper
levity, the balcony was built. Rav. Aharon Kotler *zal* ("Sanctity of the Synagogue" P. 127) makes the following *kal
vachomer.* "Now, how much greater still is the conclusion
that we must draw: if in the Temple with its great sanctity,

. . . where all fulfilled the commandment 'Thou shalt fear My Sanctuary' (Leviticus 26:2) the Sages nevertheless felt it necessary to build a balcony to separate men and women, and thus guard against improper levity, though previously they had not mingled—in our generation that is so inferior to them in all matters dealing with sanctity and the fear of G-d, as is obvious to any sensible person, it is surely a far greater necessity to separate men and women to preserve the sanctity of the synagogue."

The halachic significance of this discussion is made evident by the following ruling of Rabbi Joseph B. Soloveitchik ("Sanctity of the Synagogue" P. 110): "I do hereby reiterate the statement I have made on numerous occasions that a synagogue with a mixed seating arrangement forfeits its sancity and its halachic status of *mikdash meat* (a Sanctuary-in-miniature), and is unfit for prayer and *avodah shebelev* (the service of the heart). With full cognizance of the implications of such a Halachic decision, I would still advise every Orthodox Jew to forego *tefillah be-tzibbur* (group prayer) even on Rosh Hashana and Yom Kippur, rather than enter a synagogue with mixed pews." The lesson concludes with the words of Rabbi Soloveitchik (*ibid.*, P. 116) analyzing the role played by the *mechitza* in enabling the *mithpallel* to achieve *kavanah* in his prayer.

Temple Israel
Minneapolis, Minnesota

IN HONOR OF
THE CONFIRMATION OF
SALLY & JOHN RUBENSTEIN
FROM
BERNICE RUBENSTEIN